of the book.

I have written random things on this page because I can.

It doesn't matter what they say.

Books from real publishing houses have numbers and dates and cryptic info on these pages.

I don't.

My book is self-published.
But that's okay.

Thank you for buying it.
Hopefully, you like it.

Forgive me.

Please.

For what you read in here. It's terrible.

I've decided that I'm going to put some weird numbers at the bottom of this page, now.

They're important to me. The numbers, I mean.

AMD 11161988RMC 7261986

There. Now, it looks professional.

For my father and mother,

who loved me

when I was still so unlovable.

FOREWORD

I dreamed of writing a masterpiece ever since I was a kid but dreaming and accomplishing are two very different things. There were many times it seemed impossible, that I just couldn't do it. My passion didn't match my skill, and I was on drugs besides. People grimaced when they read what I wrote. Others told me to flat out forget about it, but finally, the book I have carried inside of myself like some metaphysical fetus for the last 31 years has been birthed upon these pages. It is a true story. It is also fictional when necessary, so that the innocent and the guilty might be protected. Besides, artistic liberties help the story flow better when it comes to recreating conversations, certain situations, internal dialogues or just trying to be funny.

The first three episodes/chapters/whatever they are show me as the child of my parents living in the city where the child grew up. The prose is consistent with that. By the time I got to San Francisco, my mind melted into the dark entity that is that great city, and life became a terrifying cartoon. The prose intends to become more fantastic and dreadful to accommodate.

The depravity progresses with each section of the book and usually spikes after any attempt to retreat from the frontlines of my sickness and insanity. I loved the Shipibos and Teo's family and tried to get better while I was with them, but by the time I got to El Callao, I was on a death mission. It plays out like a cinematic thriller: A Story of Love, Cocaine and Murder in the Streets of Peru.

Turtle Tom presents a lot of things for readers to consider, some laughs and disgusted head shaking. Danielle was a willing participant in one of my most drug addled and violent experiments, a devoted partner through a ruthless time of my life. She bore the brunt of my recklessness for a time, but she is not innocent.

The section about the epidural abscess and MRSA is factually based and told in a matter of fact manner. Dreezy represents the decline in standards and my mental health. I loved her, and by that time of the book, I'm completely comfortable, although miserable, being a homeless and criminal dope fiend. That was who I was in Portland at 26, consummating the transformation that began in San Francisco at 19 years old. A savage lost.

It aspires to have all the danger and excitement of a 16th century explorer's journal through the American wilderness. It is the shameful reflection of a repentant sinner's evil deeds. It hopes to be as sappy as a Lifetime Original made for TV movie and absurd as any installment of Monte Python. It mocks the ridiculous notions of my former self and never flinches at the indecency of an addict. Somewhere in there is the mixture of my father's voice and my 16-year-old self on his skateboard, bleeding and screaming profanities.

I will tell you of horrible things. I will tell you of great love. I will tell you of divine intervention and supernatural power and the awkward boredom spanning the distances in between. So, if you will, please allow me to paint the portrait of my despair and the life I eventually found. The only paints on my pallet are pain and fragmented memories from so long ago. My heart breaks as I bleed and pour myself out onto the canvas. It won't take long.

I dreamed it would be a masterpiece.

New Orleans
Summer 2004

When I was little they called me pig. Not a pig. Not the pig. But pig. And so I was. Fat. Selfish. Nasty. Whether I became those things because of what they called me or I was already that way, I don't know. But I do know that he is who I became. Over the years I would try to kill him in different ways.

My dad came to get me out of a crack house at 6 on a Monday morning, because he had not seen me since I left for school the Monday morning before. His bike was missing besides. It was my girlfriend who told him where I was. That week I rode the bike up and down Adams Street from the crack house to see her, and I made out with her on the red brick steps of her mom's house between smoking Marlboro Lights. I told her I had some heroin. She pressed her lips together and opened her eyes big as if to say,

"Okay. What do you want me to say about that? That is scary."

The rest of the week I had been with my friend Andrew in his basement apartment a few blocks from her house. That first night at his place the powders in my nose and smoke in my lungs turned on biochemical faucets in my head. My body buzzed, and my skin tingled. Only minutes seemed to have passed since we first started partying that evening, but the sun rose on us. We laughed at each other in the warm light coming through the window. The night was gone, and we would never get it back. Years later Andrew died of an overdose. Then his life was gone, and he never got it back.

I recognized my father's voice at the door before I woke up. It was steady, like he had collected himself the moment before he knocked. He came to take me back home. The drugs I did the night before still swirled bliss in the black behind my eyelids. A hand touched my shoulder. The urgent whispers of someone standing over me in the dark startled me awake.

"Riley! Riley! Wake up! Your dad is here!"

Where was I? What was I doing here? Where were my drugs?

Andrew directed my father to his bike and he grabbed it and went back outside to load it into the Land Cruiser before I was collected enough to speak. While he was outside, I turned to Andrew.

"Turn on the light! I have to find my heroin. I had five foils last night." The light emitted by the filament burned my retinas. I shielded my eyes.

"Are you sure? I don't remember that, dude. Where would it be?" I found a large bindle of cocaine in my pocket.

Probably a gram and a half, but it wasn't heroin. I wanted my heroin.

"I don't know. Let me check the couch. I know I had them smoking crack with Joel last night." We pulled up the cushions and found nothing. My father stood in the door after a minute, and we gave up. The engine ran in the street waiting to take me home. It was the morning after Mother's Day.

"Come on, Riley! Let's go!"

"Go with your dad. Call me later. I'll keep looking for it." Andrew turned the lights back off, and across the street, concrete crosses in a graveyard made black silhouettes against the pale morning sky. My father never said anything on the ride home, or at least nothing I can remember.

At the house my sisters and mother got dressed and ready for another regular Monday before school. I walked up to my room, and my skin crawled in desperation at the prospect of sobriety.

I pulled the tin foil bindle of cocaine out of my pocket and laid it under the lamp on my bedside dresser. It looked like a gram and a half of coke, but when I gummed it and rubbed it on my lips and tongue, it didn't numb me up. The cocaine was no good, so I chopped all of it up and snorted it all in one line. It burned badly, but as soon as it hit the back of my throat, I knew it was several times a lethal dose of heroin. It was the stuff we called China white.

It excited me to taste the heroin, because I wanted to slip into oblivion. The smallest amount of China white would put me out for several hours, an amount so small I could hardly see it when I bought it, but now I had just snorted as much as my sinus cavities could hold. Any thoughts of my own death fell away under the waves of enthusiasm I felt about how high I would soon be.

I walked downstairs to get some juice. My father cooked breakfast. The smell of bacon fat filled the kitchen.

"Poppa, I want some orange juice. Can we go get some?" He poked the bacon popping in the frying pan with a fork. His left hand rested in his pocket, and I looked around in the refrigerator.

"Not right now. Go upstairs and go to sleep in the TV room."

Ten minutes later my little sister found me. Green vomit covered my clothes and most of the couch. The dying blood in my face turned my complexion gray, and my eyes rolled all the way back into my head. She ran to get my father, who had just returned from buying orange juice.

As a veterinarian he knew how to resuscitate, so he got on his knees and pumped my chest with his hands. A large glob of brown snot ejected from my nostrils, but vomit still blocked my airway. He sucked it into his mouth and spat it out to help me breathe. With bile on my lips, he put his mouth to mine and blew in breath. He could have breathed for me for days, but the amount of heroin in my system meant certain death.

On that Monday morning before school, my sisters waited on the front porch for the ambulance. My mother shook, doubled over in the doorway, and watched her husband attempt to keep her only son alive. My father breathed for me and pushed on my chest. I lay on the ground dying, just like I wanted. My lungs started to shut down, and soon my heart would quit pumping. seventeen years into this life, and I was already on my way out. How could I do that to my mother and father? How could I do that to my sisters? How could I do that to myself?

When I was a kid, my father used to ride bikes with me down the levee to throw rocks into the river at sunset, and during his workdays, he packed me around in the passenger seat of his Land Cruiser while he made calls to clients. Everywhere we went everyone knew him and wanted his attention. They said, "Hey, Doc! Hey, Doc! Hey, Doc!" We went to different horse barns and properties throughout the countryside. One night we hooked a chain to his front bumper and tried to pull a dead calf out of its mother as it got dark outside and afterwards he let me have a sip of his beer in the back of the Land Cruiser. I used to ask him every question I had, and he always knew the answer. He was the smartest man in the world.

At some stables, he pointed and said, "A horse kicked me in the knee, and I cried under that tree." I didn't believe him, because my dad never cried. At his clinic he oversaw everything and everyone. One evening a man got shot in the head in a hunting accident on the bayou, and my dad sucked the bloody foam out of his throat until help came. The guy eventually died, but not while my dad was working on him.

He led me on a horse when I was four. It was so clear to me that he loved me in that moment and laid down his life for mine. One time I had an awful cough, and he stayed up with me to give me medicine and make sure I was okay. My very first memory is me on his hairy chest, waking from sleep, to choke back chunks of toddler vomit. He had taken a break from putting together some crawler or toy for me to drink a beer and read on the chaise lounge under a lamp. I was his only baby boy once upon a time, and he held me in his arms.

But now he knelt over me and pumped my chest with both of his hands and breathed for me, while he waited for the ambulance he hoped would come fast enough to save me.

The paramedics and firemen tried to get me to walk downstairs to the ambulance and go to the hospital. I tried to bite them. At the hospital, I spewed green vomit all over the floor and ripped the IVs out of my arm and tried to get water out of a sink. Baldheaded children gawked at my antics, and others lay silent and unconscious in the ICU. I survived.

Everyone thought it was an intentional overdose, but I didn't know what to say. It was no fun dealing with accusations of suicide. My mother's father, Turkey, sat in a chair next to me, and I gave him a hard time about them not allowing me any water. I asked him if he wanted me to vomit in his mouth. He laughed at me. The old man called me Turkey like I had called him Turkey since I was three years old. He used to wake up before the sun to drink vodka in the 1970s, but in that hospital room he had 28 years sober.

This seems like a crazy thing, some kind of big deal, and it was to us at the time, especially my family. I was just getting started, though. Overdosing was the first of many incidents and accidents that would put my life in jeopardy. My poor father and mother would watch me tear my life apart time and again. They would worry and cry over me. Eventually, it became a fact that even if I lived through my addiction, anger and chemicals had warped my mind. Whoever I was before drugs was not who I would ever be again. The next ten years would be a fight for my life, a fight I knew I couldn't win. My family was strapped in for the ride. I was the lunatic driving.

Baton Rouge
Late Fall 2004

College was no place for a person like me. Piles of clothes covered the floor of my dorm room and stank. At night I smoked crack on the other side of Roosevelt Avenue or hung out with the other kids on campus to smoke weed. Girls brought me to their dorm rooms around LSU's campus and when they fell asleep, I robbed them. I skipped classes and stayed in bed all day and made a gun with my fingers and fired it against the side of my head or into the roof of my mouth, imagining all the different ways my brains and blood would splatter on the walls. Too bad I didn't have a gun. My class attendance waned to nothing. My second and last time attending chemistry class, I pulled the scab of a cigarette burn off my hand. Thick puss leaked onto my desk. The girl who watched me do it turned me down for a date, and it wasn't long before I had a gun in my face in the ghetto. Like I said college was no place for a person like me.

After the overdose my parents had put me in rehab in Baton Rouge after my overdose, and I spent two months there. There were family therapy sessions where the counselor made my sisters and parents tell me one by one what it was like to find me overdosed on that Monday morning. The girls and my mother struggled to tell their side of the story through their tears and sobbing and hand flapping, but when my dad's turn came he grabbed a Kleenex and put it to his face. He squeezed air out of his mouth to imitate the sound of a nose blowing, and the Kleenex fluttered out in front of him. It was hilarious, and even though it was not the time for jokes, the whole room laughed. When they left I cried my eyes out, because I couldn't figure out what was wrong with me or why I did the things I did. Even worse was the fact that I wasn't getting better, and I knew it.

After the 60 days of inpatient treatment I lived in a halfway house and entered my first year of college at LSU. I went to AA meetings to appease my family or fulfill the requirements of the halfway house I lived in for a week before I left one night and never came back. The meetings were warm and crowded. There was a certain amount of hopelessness served up with the piping hot coffee in Styrofoam cups, a warm hopelessness, but hopelessness nonetheless. At least we were not alone, and we could talk about it. Don't get me wrong, plenty of people had good things to say, but when they spoke all I heard was, "If you want to stay sober like me, you just have to stick your head in our special 12step, AA-certified vise and crank it tight, until your brains slide out of your ears like mashed potatoes."

After the halfway house, I lived at my grandmother's but ended up living in an all-male dormitory on campus after I relapsed at her house. I spent most of my afternoons and nights in the courtyard of the Pentagon, a collection of five dormitories near mine. We all smoked weed or took some pharmaceuticals but none of my university friends had any idea about the crack I smoked just a few blocks away. My friend Dillon and I used to get stoned and have crazy conversations.

"Have you ever done shrooms and laid back and looked at the stars like this and thought, 'Hey, the mushroom I just took was doing this exact same thing before it got picked. You know? Just chilling out and staring up at the stars from the grass?'"

"No. That's funny." He laughed.

"I love shrooms."

"Yeah. They're pretty fun. I know some cow pastures we can probably get into."

I was excited about finding the fungus growing in the cow patties, but we found ourselves smoking crack in a trap house in the ghetto instead. We must have taken Xanax.

Soon we rode to campus with one of the dealers who called himself Lil Stanky and obtained 500 dollars' worth of high-grade marijuana from our friend named Sam back on campus to trade for an ounce of powder cocaine. The marijuana disappeared, but Stanky kept giving us hits of crack. We rode around smoking crack all night, and he told us to pull up under a tree by a house at 7 a.m. A jungle of weeds and unchecked vegetation grew all around the apparently empty neighborhood.

"I'm a run in real quick and get this issue." Issue meant ounce, and that was common knowledge in the neighborhood they called "the Bottoms." I have visited ghettos in the Third World and across the United States, and I am sure that some places are actually worse than "the Bottoms." I've just never found one.

A cold piece of metal pushed into the base of my skull. It was not completely unexpected, and Stanky pushed my head forward with it. He told us to get out of the car and put our hands on the hood while he searched us. Then, he followed us into the empty house where old wires hung from between the joists of the ceiling, and a tree grew up through the broken floor and back out through the old window. Stanky had lagged out of earshot trying to hold his pistol and hit the pipe before he walked into the doorway.

But for the occasional chirps of birds in the early morning light we stood in silence, and I asked Dillon if he thought we would die. Dillon's lips straightened, and his face was green. He couldn't speak. We would be murdered right there, and we both knew it. I probably should have thought about things like how long it would take authorities to find our bodies in such a desolate part of the ghetto or when my mom would realize that I was missing. Instead I could only think of another hit.

From the doorway Stanky accused us of ripping him off, even though it was the other way around. I talked him down and offered him some of the powder that we had purchased from him earlier in the night. It was in a paper bindle in my sock, and he got close enough to snatch it from me while keeping the gun pointed at us. He snorted bumps through each nostril off his long pinky nail and folded the bindle up before he gave it back.

"Aight. We cool. Get back in the car."

The pistol pointed at the back of my skull, and Dillon drove for the first few hours. Stanky made us buy him cartons of cigarettes with our campus credit cards, and then he drove and put me in the back and Dillon in the front. It was more annoying than scary after a while, except for when he drove us down desolate dead ends in that ghetto and parked. Stanky would blast the speakers of Dillon's sound system. His chest would heave. His eyes would open wide and wild, with his trigger finger squirming. Dillon would turn the knob way down and say,

"It's cool, man! It's cool! You don't want to do that!"

After we would talk him out of murdering us we would go buy him another carton of cigarettes which he would trade for crack that he smoked with us, but one time he recruited an old wiry guy named Leroy pushing a broken lawn mower down the street to pull Dillon's last 40 bucks out of an ATM. Leroy agreed, but when he came back from the ATM he said that there were only $20 in the account. Stanky didn't believe him, so we all went in together and found the receipt of the last transaction hanging out of the ATM. It said that $40 had been withdrawn, and we spent the next hour talking Stanky out of killing Leroy. It was almost funny, and from the wrong end of Stanky's gun barrel we began to bond with him.

As the reader you might expect something more profound from me as the writer, but I don't have anything to offer. It was simply the life I lived back then, and this was the natural progression of things in that environment and with that kind of chemical dependency. If there was anything to say about it, it was that only a few years separated me from Stanky but we came from worlds that existed light years apart. He smoked crack and found himself in the middle of an armed-robbery type of situation because it was everything he knew. Those were the values and the trajectories of men in his life and neighborhood. I found myself in the same situation, albeit on the other side of the pistol, but I was there after wholesome values and every opportunity in the world had been handed to me. I was there because I wanted to be. He didn't have as many choices about it.

Stanky loaded hits of crack into his pipe and passed it to us while we rode around the ghetto. We laughed at the things and people we saw. He bought us beer and Valium from an old man selling his prescriptions outside of a corner store. It was about 11 when Stanky parked under a tree by the LSU lakes and made us dismantle the amps in Dillon's car to repay him for the fictitious drug deal gone wrong.

"Dude! I'm supposed to be taking my Dairy Science midterm right now!"

Neither of them seemed to care about my problems as Dillon gritted his teeth and complained about the situation and threatened me because I kept asking for hits of crack, and Stanky wanted us to hurry. All I could think about was another hit, but in fact, I intended to major in biology at LSU and studied to be a veterinarian when I wasn't being a crackhead in the ghetto.

I would have failed the exam anyway. Taking the midterm would have only been my third time coming to class, and I never bought the textbook in the first place. (On the day of the Dairy Science final I walked all the way to the building but passed up the classroom door and went to the bathroom instead of taking the test. That's how I was.)

We continued to ride around with Stanky, and six hours after he first pressed the gun into the back of my head Stanky stopped the car and put it in park and let it idle. He looked at us and nodded.

"Don't come looking for me. Happy Thanksgiving."

Dillon and I had a fake story because we had to account for the fact that we didn't want people to know we were trying to score drugs and smoking crack when we got held up. It made it seem more like it was our fault if we were smoking crack, and we wanted sympathy. My parents wanted me to report it to the police. The cops laughed at us and refused to even start paperwork. I failed Dairy Science and dropped out of school a few months later, but I saw Stanky often after that. When I needed powder for one of the other college kids, he handled it for me. He always wanted to know about Dillon.

"How's old boy doing?" he used to ask.

New Orleans
Summer 2005

It is true that I survived Hurricane Katrina with my father in New Orleans, and that before our two months together were over, he threatened to shoot me with a 9-millimeter. But before I tell you about that, I need to tell you about my girlfriend from high school, and that whole thing starts with a large shipment of blotter acid that came into the city at the very end of 2003. It was printed with pink elephants on a purple background. Supposedly it came from the Lavender family, whatever that meant, and it made an unlikely couple out of us.

My family and I were out of town for Christmas break of my senior year, but I can't remember where we went. I think it was Mexico, and while we were gone, the captain of the cheerleading team from high school took some of that acid with two of my friends. They tried to come see me, but we were gone. Somehow their journey to find me and my absence mixed with the LSD to simulate feelings of love and longing for me in her. When I got back, this girl I barely knew, the captain of the cheerleading team, wanted to hang out with me.

After I failed out of LSU and toward the end of our relationship, I stole $200 out of her purse, money which she was holding for one of our friends and disappeared for 24 hours with her vehicle. When I came back we screamed at each other. Later she dropped me off at my parents' house, and I hurled my cellphone at the pavement in the driveway under the oak tree. Its bark bloodied my knuckles when I punched it, and I thought the bones might have broken in my hands and wrist. Inside of the house my parents and I screamed before they told me to leave and locked me out. They called the police. I stuck my fist through the window in a door on the front porch and turned the old knob to let myself in. When the cops showed up I was eating a hot dog.

"Put the hot dog down! You are under arrest!"

But it all of this didn't start out like that for the cheerleader and me. The first time we hung out, I took two of those pink elephants, and the Jimi Hendrix coming out of her speakers seemed to cause my brain to leak out of my eyes and nose. It puddled itself in an awkward Technicolor mess on my shirt. She kept her cool and comforted me as I tried to clean it up. We rode to school every morning after that and knew each other in ways that no one else did. The girl shed tears over my addiction and wrote privately in a journal about how much she loved me when we were out with friends.

After my overdose and the episode with Stanky and the rest of our miserable 18 months together, she had enough. She moved on, and the breakup played out in my head every second. It was like a smoldering heap of twisted metal and mental torment, like a train wreck of my own emotions and the memories we created together. I staggered. I struggled to breathe. I fell to my knees. Images of her smile and the love she once held in her eyes faded away in front of me like smoke slowly dissipating or the mirage of a desert oasis I would never reach.

I punched myself in the face until I had two black eyes. I called her 50 times a day. While she was working once, I wrote a poem to tell her how pathetic I was and left it on her windshield in a psychotic spider's web of scotch tape, but I never got her back. I lost her forever, and I only had myself to blame.

Anyway, that gives you an idea of how things were going for me around the time Katrina came to town, but I should also tell you about the job my uncle gave me. It was delivering trays of medical instruments and every kind of orthopedic implant to different hospitals for the company representatives and the surgeons they did business with. I disappeared into the ghetto in the middle of a delivery one afternoon and would not answer my phone. Somehow the $70,000 dollars' worth of medical equipment ended up where it was supposed to go, but I disappeared to my friends' house that night. In the morning, my uncle called to tell me he didn't want me to give up on life.

My cell phones never had a voicemail message, but if they did, it would have said something like, "Hi, you've reached Riley. I'm not able to take your call right now, because I am smoking crack. Leave your name and number, and I'll be sure to ignore it, until I need something from you. Thanks."

That brings us right up to the account of the hurricane because my friends only let me stay with them for a few days before they evacuated for Katrina. My mom picked me up from their house and took me home to help my dad board up the windows. They waited out the storm at the house. I stayed with my grandmother and my uncle who had just given me that job and and his two kids at a hotel downtown. My ex-aunt and my uncle's new wife were there too.

The night before Katrina made landfall my cousin and I watched the satellite footage of the huge storm bearing down on the Gulf Coast just below New Orleans. My uncle had rented hotel rooms for his ex-wife, my cousins, my grandmother and me, and during the storm, the windows cracked on the 21st floor of the Loews Hotel across from Harrah's Casino. Rain could be seen ripping through the city in the currents of wind pushing through the streets, and the wire and plaster materials used to construct the exterior of other buildings fluttered in the air like pieces of tissue. There seemed to be a kind of divine wrath being poured out onto the city. At least that's what people were saying. There had been seven senseless murders in one night just before the storm.

Management fed us and moved us down to the 15th floor to another room, but the water didn't work. Eventually the storming stopped, and we made phone calls to people we cared about. I tried to call the girl whose house I slept at before she evacuated and was happy to talk to her. After that I called my mom.

"Riley! The levees broke! I need you to come get me from the house and bring me back to the hotel."

"Okay. Is Poppa coming?"

"No. He has too many animals at the clinic. I tried to talk him into it, but I don't think he will come."

"Okay. Well I should probably stay with him."

"Yeah. I think that would be best but come get me and bring me back to the hotel."

My grandmother let me take her Camry to get my mom from the house, and I went up Tchoupitoulas Street to get there. Houses sat abandoned and desperate and were vulnerable prey to the looters and pillagers running around the city. I picked my mother up at the house and headed back to the Loews down St. Charles Avenue. Men hung halfway out of cars they did not own and sweated trying to get them started. Storefront windows had holes smashed into them, but everything inside was already gone.

Back at home, our dog had puppies during the storm, and my dad told me about how he went outside to feel the wind and see what kind of damage was being done. He got locked out. My mom couldn't hear him knocking so he was out there for over an hour in the rain and wind. We camped out on the roof of the front porch that first night, but somebody at the hotel had given me some Xanax. I had $20 in my pocket and decided that I would sneak out the front of the house and take the Camry to go smoke crack.

He flashed his light on me from the front porch roof as I started the Camry and took off into the dark. No automobiles made any noise in the streets, and not one streetcar ran up or down the tracks. Telephone poles lay on the ground with their power lines tangled in messes of large live oak limbs that covered St. Charles Avenue from one end to the other. It was a dangerous prospect taking off like that into the desolate city in a small car, and it was almost impossible to get the Camry from our house on Palmer Avenue all the way to ghetto by the parish line, but I did it.

When I got to the ghetto by Leake Avenue and Oak everyone in the neighborhood converged in the streets. An atmosphere of panic hovered over us, and they darted around like bees in a hive worried they would perish. Water came out of the drains and pooled in the streets. There was a man carrying a large box fan on his shoulder in the crowd, and he had the twitch in his walk I was looking for. I flagged him down, and he ran over to the car.

"What's up, Wodee?"

"Looking for a 20."

"I got you. Let me put this in the car."

He put the fan into the back seat of my grandmother's Camry and took my 20 into a house. Historic buildings across town lay in heaps of ashes smoldering, and other buildings waited to be consumed by fire or looted. A deluge of black water destroyed whole neighborhoods where families once lived and kids once played. Pandemonium swept across the city. Those who remained realized that our beloved New Orleans was drowning, and it looked like the city might never recover even if it survived this catastrophe. I sat in the car waiting for the crack head to come back with my crack rock, and my father sat on the front porch roof of our house wondering if I would come back with the car or get killed trying to smoke crack in the chaos.

I lost the hit in the car before I could smoke it. There was nothing I could do to recover it, so I got out and tried to cut a deal with a guy who desperately needed gas. He said he would help me out, and we tried to siphon gas out of the car, but it didn't work. Since I tried to help he waved off his friend who followed us around and looked like he had his hand on a pistol in his waistband. When I got back to the house my father gave me a Tylenol PM and begged me to sleep.

In the morning the crack had worn off, and we began to navigate our stay in post- Katrina New Orleans. We parked the Camry at my dad's clinic in Jefferson Parish and rode around in the old Land Cruiser. Sometimes we picked up the displaced people walking up and down St. Charles and took them to Ochsner Hospital. There was one lady with frizzy, frazzled hair who carried a bunch of cat carriers and looked like she had lived her life as a recluse in one of the nearby neighborhoods, but the flood brought her out. When we stopped and asked her if she wanted a ride or needed help she just turned around and walked in the other direction. Sometimes we got calls at my dad's clinic from people who wanted us to break into their houses and rescue their animals, so we did.

At night we tried to sleep outside, because it was so hot. Mosquitoes hung around us in softly humming clouds and bit hard, even through our sheets drenched in Adam's Flea and Tick. I cooked some steaks over a fire but had caked the seasoned salt on them in the dark. We could barely eat them. There was a silence that filled the air and gave us a dread we had never known about the future of our lives.

The destruction of the city matched the emptiness inside of me. It was fitting for me to be there and see it all. Not that either one caused the other, but the dire straits of the city mirrored the reality of my own insides. My childhood pediatrician hanged himself over the city's devastation, while my father focused on the litter of puppies our Italian greyhound had to get through it. As if everything happening at the time wasn't enough stress for him, I gave him hell by smoking crack, stealing money and getting violent.

I found my sister's Adderall prescription and took the whole thing at once. Then I chugged warm beers we had until I couldn't talk or sleep, and I smoked crack with a pimply-skinned lady and her boyfriend in a crumbling apartment building called the Studio Arms by Ochsner Hospital. On the way back home, the cops stopped me for being out after curfew but let me go.

We spent the nights at his clinic and made trips to our house in Orleans Parish during the days. He shot the trunk of a magnolia tree with the 9-millimeter out of boredom one afternoon. On another night, two members of the National Guard robbed the house while we slept at the clinic. Both were arrested and received dishonorable discharges.

After a month my dad got me a job with a contractor who lived in nearby Harahan, and on our first job we demolished the insides of a house belonging to a man whose wife had just divorced him and left with his daughters a few weeks before the storm. In wheelbarrows we carted photo albums and mildewed art projects made of construction paper and Elmer's glue out through the front door and into a dumpster. Every single memory the man had of his daughters' childhoods had fallen under the chalky brown water line a foot below the ceiling. The man sweated and took pictures hoping his insurance company might pay him for his losses, for the things that have no price. I quit after a week.

Sometime toward the end of our time together in the shambles of a post-Katrina New Orleans my dad got on the phone to help me get the $2,300 FEMA gave to survivors of Katrina, and after that I got into it with him. It was over something stupid, but I got him in a headlock and rammed the top of his skull into the corner of a doorway behind the clinic. We struggled for a few minutes before we stopped, and he said

"You attack me like that again, Riley, and I'm gonna shoot you. You hear me?"

I knew he meant it, and he would have been right to do it with the way I acted. It reminded me of the time he told me he wanted to fight me as a teenager but remembered how much he had paid for my teeth to be straight. I tore off in the Land Cruiser up to Baton Rouge, where I stayed with my mom and sisters at my grandmother's until I could figure out what to do.

Eventually, my mother and I devised a plan for me to go live in California with my friends who had all moved out to San Francisco and planned to grow weed on Treasure Island. My mom didn't know about any of that though. They said needed another roommate to make it work, so I told them I would be out there soon. My mom bought a ticket, but it would be a week or so before I could fly out. In that last week, my friend stole a car and picked me up in the middle of the night. By the time the sun came up we were trying to buy some crack in the ghetto with a fake $100 bill, but when the dealer came back to the car, he wanted the rocks back I rolled onto my back and kicked him in the face and ground his fingers under my heel before he fell out of the back seat.

We may have run over him, but we definitely drove into a ditch before we escaped. All the while the kid in the back seat next to me snored and had his head between his legs and a strand of drool hanging from his lip to the floor. My mom had to come get me out of a crack house a few days later. It was the morning of my flight to San Francisco, and my father hadn't talked to me since we'd fought last.

San Francisco
Fall-Winter 2005

    Behold, a savage lost in the city streets. See him cower in the cold. He is pale and thin and dressed in rags. He sleeps on sidewalks and takes his meals from dumpsters. His are the eyes that peer out from beneath city bridges at night. His is the blood splattered on the bathroom walls.

    Behold, a savage lost.

I spent a few hours laid over somewhere in the Southwest and arrived at the Oakland airport late that night. My friend Roger and his girlfriend came from the city on the BART to pick me up and took for granted that I would pay for the cab ride back to their hotel room. San Francisco mystified the boy who had only read about her in books and never lived anywhere but Louisiana. This was where R. Crumb lived in the '60s and beautiful people had once worn flowers in their hair. Jack Kerouac journeyed across the United States more than once to her, chronicling the adventures in "On the Road," and here was where Ken Kesey and his Merry Pranksters held some of the first acid tests and Andre Nickatina sold crack in the Fillmore projects over his Blackberry cell phone. The city held untold adventure in her streets, and I would discover it.

At the hotel I paid the driver, and we loaded my bags into their room.

"Roger, when can you get some acid? When can we trip?" I lit a cigarette on the balcony of their hotel room on Lombard.

"Give me a light." He held his head down until he pulled smoke into his lungs. He lifted his face to me and let the smoke out of his mouth and nose. "I don't know. Maybe soon, but you need to get settled. Tomorrow we'll take you to the Red Cross to get your ATM card and the hotel room. We're tired."

In the morning we went and got things settled. I put my $2,300 from FEMA in the Bank of America and got a $300 ATM card from the Red Cross and a room in a hotel next to one of our friends from New Orleans. Pretty soon we would all move in together and grow weed, and I felt great hope and excitement about starting over and leaving behind the wreckage of New Orleans. I could reinvent myself and do amazing things, but when Roger and his girlfriend stayed in my room one night, we all took Xanax. I journeyed to the Tenderloin to smoke crack and walked back to the room to steal $200 from Roger's girlfriend while she slept.

My legs hurt from walking up and down the hills on Market between Seventh and Church, and when I got back to the room at 7 o'clock, Roger woke up and went into the bathroom. The clouds of steam and white noise came through the crack in the door, and his girlfriend looked frantically through her purse for her wallet.

"Where's my wallet? Where is it?!?"

I stood sweaty in the corner with my shoes on like someone who had been smoking crack all night, and she looked confused and then like she hit Bingo and then like she smelled excrement. She walked into the bathroom to tell Roger that I took her money. I threw her empty wallet behind the nightstand, and when she came out I asked,

"Oh, is this it? What's it doing here?" She didn't say anything when I handed it to her, and they left. Roger banged on the door to wake me up in the dark a few hours later.

"Dude! You better give her that money back!"

"Dog! You know I got the money. It's in the bank. I'll go tomorrow morning when they open. First thing, and I'll give her 20 bucks extra. I'm sorry, bro. Xanax does me like that. You know how I get."

"Yeah. I know. She's mad. So, tomorrow?"

"First thing. I promise. The banks aren't open right now. Tell her I'm sorry."

I was on my own. They didn't want to grow weed with me anymore. They didn't want to live with me either, and I couldn't blame them. I had no idea what to do with myself if my plans with them fell through.

Roger sold me a sheet of acid, and that put my bank account at something like $1,300 down from the original $2,300 after one week in California. I slipped into the fog of a mind laced with acid and watched VH1 videos play all night. Sheryl Crow's "Good Is Good" video played over and over, and there was a knock at the door by daylight. I opened to discover the wiry frame of a man I had smoked crack with a few nights before, and I let him in. We smoked a bunch more for the next few days. I stole 40 bucks from him when he passed out, to go smoke some more before the banks opened, but when I came back, he woke up.

"I'm not leaving till you get me my money!"

"No problem. I have money in the bank. Just let me go get it." I left the room with my jacket, my skateboard, my passport, my phone and the promise to pay him back.

Everything else I owned was in that room, but when I found out that the banks were closed for Columbus Day, I knew I was screwed. The only things I found in the room when I got back 12 hours later were the sheet of acid in the drawer and a streak of feces on my pillow case. The Cambodian maid who cleaned my room chastised me for getting robbed and told me how she had tried to stop the guy. It seemed to hurt her to see me controlled by drugs, but that was life for me. I never thought about it much.

After that I smoked meth in my hotel room and went to sell the sheet of acid with one of the street people I had met. My accomplice sent me into the store to buy a Three Musketeers bar for him while he waited for the buyer in the parking lot, but when I came out he was gone. The candy bar was pitiful consolation for the loss of the LSD; my mouth was too dry from meth to eat it. There was no milk, and I hated nougat besides.

Back in my room, a man who dressed like the Terminator spoke dark poetry and injected meth into my arm with a needle that he pulled out of his boot. It was the first time I used it much and still had not learned how to shoot myself up. I also didn't know where to score, but the sociopath in black leather did. Hits of quality crank hammered my mind into hamburger meat, and I lost it.

I hallucinated. Thick plumes of angry smoke rose into a blood-soaked sky. The earth underfoot howled for the desolation that sat upon her. Black messengers of death squawked at me from the air. My hotel sat on a beach in Florida, and strange junkies and random speed freaks owned the room. It was not mine anymore but theirs. Large men with stubble, breasts, beautiful hair and acne laughed like donkeys neighing and passed meth pipes around the room. I cowered in the corner, my mind feeble and fragmented. Sometimes I stood barefoot in the cold and watched the insanity unfold through the window, the infancy of a new day laying the first layers of its blue luminescence on everything. I begged them to let me in out of the cold.

I woke up to an old episode of "COPS" flickering blue on the silent TV. It seemed as if the room was filled with a cloud of bad breath and meth smoke. The lampshades hung crooked off their posts with random articles of clothing partially blocking the light. The man in black leather and a couple of other people I didn't recognize hung off the bed and chairs like wet dish towels. Management kicked me out as soon as they saw me.

The Red Cross put me up in a hotel room in Chinatown, and I spent a week floating around with a pair of bolt cutters and a guy who couldn't decide if his name was Chet or Chad. He always insisted that he wasn't my homeboy and that I ought to quit referring to him as such. One day I came back to the hotel and found white silhouettes on the wall where the TV and dresser once sat. The phone had been ripped out of the wall, and the mattress was gone too. Turned out, he wasn't my homeboy after all.

I disappeared into the streets. Three times people had robbed me of all I had in just three weeks away from home. My mind was still reeling from the trauma of that first IV meth binge, and there was nowhere go in a big and scary city.

Really being homeless scared me. And within the first few hours into it my father called me. We hadn't really talked since that day that we got into it at the clinic, and all he had heard of me was what my friends told him about me using the needle. He told me that he, my sister and my mother had been in a head-on collision going to his mom's house on Thanksgiving Day. He said that they were in ambulances and that his arm hurt, my mom's neck was broken and my sister had amnesia. I got the phone call by Civic Center Plaza, where this man on roller skates wore a pair of sunglasses and denim short shorts and headphones. He danced in a state of drug-induced euphoria. My heart broke, and I felt such pain and fear. I bawled right there in front of everyone, and the man on roller skates stopped to give me a puzzled look, as if to say, "These are the streets, man. We don't do that here."

I became a particle of dust floating in the dark below skyscraper monsters, and the city was an organism. We walked her streets like sludge sliding through her veins and a sickness in her bones. We were a wandering hollow-eyed horde. I stood atop a hill at night studying her lights and whispered, "As the city sleeps. As the city sleeps. Hell crawls through her streets."

I wrote poetry. It said things like, "Do you like to get your fix? Do you like to hit licks? Do you like dirty rigs? Because I got six in each one of my pockets. This ain't the life that anyone picks. We're just kids out here, trying to get our tricks." Pedestrian mobs waiting to cross turned into audiences, entertained by my screaming and one-sided conversations on a big blue shoe or daring and technical skateboard exhibitions. I introduced myself to strangers as RC Dizzle Wizzle and danced like a maniac on street corners for all to see. The city seemed a dark and drug addled playground to me sometimes.

Down at the open-air insane asylum called the Tenderloin, an angry black man held a pimply and bald-headed Filipino by the neck against a wall, pimping him out to passersby. I saw a 300-pound transsexual sitting on a crate between two cars and servicing another man who smoked his crack pipe freely once. A block down Golden Gate was where we sat our backs to a chain link fence and injected our drugs. On Market and 7th were Mexican and Asian fences (guys who bought our stolen goods to resell for a profit later). They bought two cans of instant coffee for five bucks. Men walked up and down Leavenworth and Turk calling out whatever drug they had for sale, and in the 24-hour Carl's Jr. another transsexual used a pair of tweezers to pick at her eyebrow-shaped scabs and looked intently into her pocket mirror. I refused her offer to eat the squishy grapes rolling around in the dirty grocery bag on the table. Another man asked me what JFK was doing in the Tenderloin and laughed. Men and women walked by spouting gibberish like radios scrolling through the dial. Others waited in silence for Skynet to take over.

Mission and 16th was about the same in terms of drugs and insanity, and I learned to spend my days and nights fooling the front desks of the welfare hotels to get out of the rain. Damp stairwells gave me a place to turn the crook of my arm into a pincushion privately as I taught myself to register blood. Staph and schizophrenia crawled on the walls, and I sat in wonder that people lived in places like this before I realized that it would have been a step up from where I was in life. Sooner or later hotel management would find me and scream at me in a foreign language until they pushed me out of the front gate and back into the elements.

A certain societal imbalance marked all my dealings and time in the city of San Francisco. It was a place where men's consciences went unchecked by the influence of females, because they had long since cast off the standards of moral decency demanded by their mothers, sisters, daughter or what were now sure to be estranged wives. There are advantages that come from such complete moral abandon, and it isn't hard to figure out what a 19-year-old homeless dope fiend does to survive in that environment. He does the kind of things that involve old men getting on their knees behind some back-alley dumpster before they spit their dentures out and press their foreheads into the young man's belly button. Gagging and choking and slobbering and handing over a $20 bill. I was no stranger to those things, and I lost a bit of myself every time.

On another night a beautiful and slender Asian lady, maybe 25 years old, found me in the rain. She wore a tight black dress, delicate and distressed. I crouched with my back against the wall of her building's front door entrance when our eyes met. I desperately desired the touch of a woman after so much time in

San Francisco. She was beautiful, and her eyes said it all so I stood up to kiss her by the door.

I knew where I was and what that might mean about her and for me. But I was so thirsty for the taste of a woman's lips and hungry for soft skin. Her perfume filled my nostrils. As soon as we kissed I knew it wasn't what I had hoped, but long hair between my fingers and her breasts in my hands sold me on the deal.

Inside of the apartment, her penis was a great disappointment, but we made the most of it. In the morning she gave me a $5 bill and sent me back into the freezing rain. It was about 10 o'clock, and I took shelter in a KFC where I bought some chicken and a biscuit.

After two months of hard living on the streets my dad came to visit and we rented a car to drive down the coast. We saw Cannery Row and ate at a restaurant where he talked to the waiter about getting an education in California. He bought me a new skateboard, a Northface hiking bag and a Kangol cap. It was weird to have him there and for him to watch me interact with the homeless junkies throughout the city.

He smoked weed with me where Haight Street runs into Golden Gate Park, and I threatened the life of a guy who had ripped me off some weeks before. After that I tried to show my dad how to take the bus while we were stoned and how I got around the city as a homeless person. He had money, and he didn't want to take the bus so he called a cab that took us back to the room. Sometimes marijuana will show you the way things really are, and the way things really were that night was too much for him. He wanted to go home that night. He wanted to get out of the nightmare that I was living in. After three days of trying not to be too disappointed and making the most of it, he gave me $200 and told me that he loved me before he took off in a cab to the airport. I think I went to Mission and 16th with the money.

After the visit and the never-ending bombardment of men who wanted sex from me, I wanted a regular friend and found one. Cody came across me in the middle of the street, delirious and struggling to skateboard. It was 4 a.m. He took me back to his squat on Guerrero between 14th and 15th and traded me one of two grape-sized balloons of heroin for a bag of weed I had, even though he didn't smoke. I tore the package open with my teeth and melted the morsel of black goo into a small puddle of coffee-colored magic. We talked between bouts of blissful slumber.

It was odd inside of his room, like we had crawled through a doorway in his eardrum and into his mind riddled with holes. In the ether of his room, we went back in time to when punk turned into grunge. He was the same kid who had run away from home at 14 in black combat boots and the denim jacket with spikes and sleeves cut off. Even though he was 33 now, he saw himself the way he was in 1991. All that he could see he stole. Cody filled up his garage-like room with useless electronics and other things he scavenged from doorsteps around the city. He squawked every word he spoke and had purple track marks that ran up and down his arms and neck like the stitched seems of a stuffed drawstring doll. His wood-glued Mohawk fit perfectly with the chain from his septum to his earlobe, and pinprick pupils revealed his ravaged soul. Preoccupation with heroin eclipsed everything else. He didn't seem to notice his teeth were gone or that the last 15 years had passed. I was 19, and I wanted to be just like him.

We sniffled. We yawned. We ached until we fixed up. Then we bombed down hills at night on our skateboards. The shiny hood ornaments of vandalized cars jangled on the chains hanging from our waists. We howled and barked like dogs at the people walking by and tore through traffic on wet streets in the fog. Falling meant dying, and we pushed it harder every chance we got. We hung off the back bumpers of trucks heading up the hills like skiers on a lift and ripped back down the pavement.

Sometimes we sat on Mission and 16th so he could play guitar and let his voice echo in the empty dark between buildings. Zombie crack heads laughed at his singing and the sight of us. We were invincible and intimidating as Vikings all night long but when the sun came up, we came down. Then, our backs hurt and we rode the ferry to work, where we groaned through painful labor regretting every moment of the night before. In the evening, we rode back to the city with runny noses. We got our fix and did it all over again.

The city was my mother, and I was her child, an infant formed in the rancid womb of the whore and birthed into heartlessness. She had no milk for me to drink. She had no love to give because cold concrete and sidewalks cannot nurture you. They can only make you hard.

I knew another guy who lived on the third floor of the King George Hotel on Market by Church. When Cody and the goons that lived in his squat had enough of me I would spend the night at the King George. The guy was a witch and one of the guys who always tried to get me to have sex with him. Once I crashed out for three days and nights after a runner. The few times I woke up he passed burning incense over me and did incantations. He told me that burning jasmine brought unity between people, but I didn't believe him or care.

"I'm a witch, you know that, right?" He asked me with a feminine and conceited wag of the head.

"No. Don't you mean warlock, or something? Aren't witches usually women?" I was pretty sure that women were witches, but he seemed feminine enough. Who was I to say what he was anyway? I didn't know.

"No. I'm a witch. See my altar?" He pointed to a glass table on the side of his TV with large rocks and crystals, a mortar and pestle, odd figurines made of shiny metal and crumbling arrangements of earthy herbs. He told me about how he cursed some woman for touching his altar against his wishes and how she was afraid of him after that. "I got a picture of her head and put it in my mirror box, and then next time I saw her, she was terrified of me."

He asked me to get him a $20 bag of meth one night, which went wrong, and the whole incident reminds me of this joke. Instead of keeping plans or being on time, meth addicts would rather spend the week trying to turn the toaster into a time machine and go back in time to keep their missed obligations. We called our inability to keep appointments or distinguish 30 minutes from three days tweeker time. I was as guilty of it as anyone.

But like I was saying, the witch wanted me to score for him, so I came over, left my stuff in his room and took off on my skateboard. He seemed upset when I showed up three days later with a perfectly good excuse and 60 dollars' worth to make up for it, and in front of the many pedestrians he screamed loudly about our deal and the drugs I had on me. I grabbed his collar and pulled his nose close until it touched mine, politely instructing him to "shut the f*ck up!'

He broke free and ran up to his apartment. I skated down the hill and found Cody, who helped me sell a 20 out of the 60. Then I did the rest of it and hid my mind in a cloud of murderous thoughts. At some point I called him about the incident to tell him I would have the money in the morning, but he threatened to keep the things my father gave me on his visit and said he would never give them back.

It was 8 o'clock when his hotel opened for visitors, and I checked in with management first thing. On the third floor of the King George his door swung open with a touch of my finger to reveal him laid out on his bed and various bottles of malt liquor around the room. I threw the 20 at his head and told him,

"There is your 20 back. I'm getting my stuff and I'm out. See you later!" He woke up.

"What? It's my birthday!" There was a hurt in his voice, probably from all the times I turned him down for sex.

"I'm getting my stuff and I'm out. Your 20 is in your bed with you."

He jumped to his feet and tried to stab me in the head with a brass letter opener, but I ducked, and he over swung. It was too easy to beat him up after he had fallen backward into my arms like that.

I made a figure four with my legs around his torso and ratcheted it tight to squeeze the air out of him. The bones in my wrists and forearms caught him at the gum and scraped up into his nose and over his entire face. Porcelain figurines crashed with the glass shelves by his TV and altar. He turned right, and I beat him in the face with my right fist and forearm. He turned left to get a beating that way too. It was his mistake to try keeping the things my father gave me. I thought I would kill him. When he tried to call the police, I took the cell phone from him and threw it out of the third-story window. He screamed and tried to bite a chunk of meat out of my forearm. The neighbors called the cops before I jumped off him and sat in the hallway waiting for the police.

The cops pulled him out of the room to show me what I did to him. Dark red tomatoes covered his face. Drying blood had run down his chin and neck from his mouth. His nose was purple and badly broken. The cops let me go. After all, I was a Katrina refugee. That's what they called me. He had everything I owned in the world in his room and tried to keep it, so I almost killed him. But the cops let me get most of it before they told me to leave and never come back.

The landlords of Cody's squat evicted us. There was no place for me to stay so I bounced around town until I got a phone call one day. I had just spilled a cooker full of goofballs (meth and heroin mixed) on the side of a shopping cart in the Central Business District before the police hassled us. The cop said he got a call about us openly using needles on the sidewalk and that he was there to check it out. My friend pulled out his syringe and demonstrated how he used it to suck the purple fluid out of the sores that covered his legs. Revolted by what he saw, the cop's chin and lips quivered before he told us to take off, and I went to sit on a bench in the cold at Embarcadero. My phone rang and showed a weird 505 area code.

"Hello?"

"Hay-low, Rah Lee?"

"Yes. This is Riley. Who's this?"

"Carlos! You mom's fren."

Carlos offered me a place to stay with him in New Mexico where I could get sober and maybe go to school.

I agreed to go. Looking back, I giggle a little bit. He had no idea what he was getting into. Fact is my personal problems were a bitter mouthful of grit he would struggle to chew, much less swallow. A faceless voice to me then, he became one of my best friends, and other than my father and mother no one tried harder to get me sober and happy.

On Dec. 26 my mom came with her mother my little sister to get me off of the streets, and I met them in the lobby of one of the ritzier hotels by Union Square. They were happy to see me and seemed to think that I would look worse. Cody and I kept doing heroin during the day, and my mom let him stay in the room with me while she stayed with my sister and her mom next door. In the morning they took us to eat breakfast, and all three laughed at Cody as he nodded out and drooled at the table over his omelet, link sausages, bacon strips, hash browns with extra cheese and two scoops of chocolate-covered ice cream melting on a short stack of pancakes. My grandmother laughed hardest of all. After that, my mom bought me all new gear, and I said goodbye to Cody and my mom at the Oakland airport and left to meet Carlos in Taos.

He met me at the airport in a green military cap and corduroy pants, before he took me to get a burrito and put me up at a hotel for the night. That first night in Albuquerque, a fevered heroin darkness played the background to my dreams. A terrifying reality choked me and startled me awake in that hotel room. There was no getting a fix to make the sickness go away. I would not get well, not this time.

Santa Fe
Winter 2006

I detoxed in the back room of Carlos's house. It was sweaty and miserable and sleepless. A slight pocking of my skin had started in San Francisco, but now it was taking a turn for the worse. It started on my arm where the witch bit me, and I swore it was a curse he put on me. The rash itched and robbed me of sleep. It tortured me. It broke my already feeble mind. My legs and ankles visibly swelled, and three different doctors had no answer. What I determined to be a secondary staph infection created crusty lesions on my thighs that broke and wept when I lifted anything heavy. A round of sulfa-based antibiotics gave me some relief, but even if the rash wasn't there to plague my life, there were other things breaking me inside.

The abrupt discontinuation of my daily heroin regimen made me feel everything my body was doing. My bones' hard surfaces cut into my aching muscles, pulling and twisting every ligament. Instead of a spine with vertebrae, I had a stack of wooden Jenga blocks ready to fall. My guts gurgled when I swallowed my saliva. I imagined my brain's synaptic firings discharged heat through my ears and caused a dull aching in my eyeballs. It was as if life had become an electrically charged fence into which I was slowly being pushed.

My feet shuffled across the floor in the daytime. Articles of clothing I collected from the streets covered Carlos's back room in truly psychotic fashion. I spilled rolling tobacco all over his house and crept around the kitchen at night. His cupboard's hinges creaked while his family slept. Solidified chunks from an ancient can of Ensure stuck between my teeth, and I gagged. It was my fault for compulsively looting his dry goods cabinet and eating whatever I found in the dark.

I reeled from the horrors I lived on the streets of Frisco. Carlos's wife would talk to me about this or that while she cooked dinner, but it always ended up with her assuring me I was OK. She promised I would recover. It was like flipping through a book you knew so well, but evil was written where there had been good. Blank pages existed where maps of myself had once been drawn, and termites had turned the remaining pieces of parchment into confetti.

    I held my head in my hands.

    Who was I? What had I done? Something was wrong and worse than ever. These were the pains of metamorphosis, which I never could feel on the drugs, but when I was sober, the screams of my own mutilated conscience echoed inside of my skull.

    I thought about my father and the things I did to hurt him. I thought about my mother and how she threw herself on the bed and cried when I got arrested at the house. I thought about the failures with my girlfriend and how disgusting I was. I registered for school and moved into the Warren Inn down in Santa Fe.

    My back felt straighter with the prospect of a new life in a new environment. It was a fresh start. Sleep was possible. Pieces of my mind were coming back. I was clean. The itchy rash was going away. Spring semester started, and I had a little girlfriend, so things were looking up.

She liked me even though I had given her a Valentine's Day card with another girl's name scratched out and hers scribbled beneath it. It was hand-drawn, and I managed to rhyme violet with toilet in the poem I wrote on the inside.

I told her she was beautiful. She looked at the scars on my legs in bed. We ate her birthday dinner at a Mexican restaurant with her family a few days after that, and her grandmother laughed at everything I said.

"You're a very interesting man!" her grandmother said.

She seemed to think I was good for her granddaughter, but I smoked cigarettes. I lay on a bare mattress in the dark. I watched reruns of "Roseanne" till 4 every morning. I wanted to burn my life down and would as soon as I got the chance.

Our relationship ended as soon as I found out that my next-door neighbor could score heroin and cocaine. My dad came to visit one weekend in late February, and it was a Saturday night when I told him I was going to see the girl. It would be a good excuse to ask for 20 bucks and give me an opportunity to try scoring at the mall. When I couldn't find anything, I walked back to the Warren Inn to see if my neighbor could help me out. I had only seen him once, but he seemed like a junkie.

He opened the door a few seconds after I knocked and told me his name was Tracy. A man named Larry with big hair and leather cowboy boots had a knee brace and crutches and sat in the corner next to an empty spoon like a proud Hispanic rooster. I spoke low so my dad wouldn't hear me through the wall.

"Can you get anything?"

"You're not a cop are you? Whatever I get you, you have to do in front of me, so I know you're not a cop."

"Yeah. That's no problem. I sort of need to do it here. My dad's next door in my room."

In 10 minutes, he took my 20 bucks out to the parking lot and came right back. He dropped a black chunk in a small baggie on the nightstand next to my chair for me to see under the light. It was exciting to know that my neighbor had a solid hook-up for heroin and cocaine as Tracy handed me a spoon. I cooked it up and pulled the brown liquid through the tiny cotton filter and into my syringe.

I had not shot up heroin since I left San Francisco, and the stint of abstinence made for a dramatic effect of the drug. It was the same as before, only more intense. My blood got warm and my stomach got queasy. The constriction of my pupils, blood vessels and lungs made it feel like an elephant was stepping on my back. Breath became shallow. Words creaked out of me like bullfrog croaks and fell onto my chest. My eyelids hung heavy and swollen. My nose itched, and I got the hiccups before I puked in Tracy's garbage can. He told me to come back in the morning if I wanted more.

My dad took off that next morning like he had planned. It had not been not the best visit. Sure, I was off the streets, but when he showed up he had to take me to buy sheets for my bed. My clothes, room, hair and life in general were more disheveled than he liked to see. I spent 20 dollars he gave me on a haircut, but it looked the same when I came back. He got mad and made me get another one.

Before he left he hunched over in the wind and counted out 200 dollars for me by the Schlotzky's in the parking lot outside of my building. He bit his tongue, because it didn't look like anything was going to change with me even if he thought I was sober for the moment.

My life unraveled.

Within a week something like 300 unopened condoms littered the whole room along with heroin cookers, rubber tourniquets, baggies of cotton balls and alcohol swabs from the needle exchange in Frisco. Trash littered the floors, and a film of cigarette tar and ashes covered the windows and mirrors. Feces piled high out of the toilet that had quit working weeks before. I systematically broke into every car in the parking lot one night and kept the useless loot. There was one half of a $20 bill, three small bags of dirt weed, several briefcases full of what appeared to be dried out potting soil, a broken ironing board, and manila folders full of someone else's old resumes, among other things that were even more useless. It was all on the floor in my room that stank and stayed dark like me.

The Warren Inn was full of sad people living sad lives who barely survived on food stamps and the crumbs they had left for the month after paying rent with their SSI. That's why the cars had nothing good to steal. A crazy guy invited me into his room on the second floor of my building and read from a notebook some things he had written. There were jars of urine and feces in the corner and on my part, an eerie desire to get out of there as soon as I could.

A middle-aged woman with bad skin lived across the hall from me with her boyfriend. He had a withered hand and a limp. They got into a fight one day, and she tore off in his van. He chased her. I ran into their room and stole a pair of boots, a jacket, a sleeve of generic Chips Ahoy and a sleeve of Saltines. Later that night, I tried to dine and dash at the IHOP but gorged myself on French toast so much I couldn't run. The next morning, I shot up a syringe full of cocaine and Tracy's blood even after he told me he had Hepatitis C.

My life continued to unravel.

Another man lived in the building next to mine. Well I supposed he was a man, but there were things about him, like his breath and the texture of his skin, that made me wonder if maybe he wasn't a clump of yeast and dough somehow become sentient. His motor skills and the air of his sophistication were on par with most 3-year-old kids I knew, and his dress only added to it: an old bomber jacket, cowboy boots, ear muffs and a pair of ski goggles to ride the bus. His only teeth stuck out from his bottom gums, like two pieces of corn.

I told him about growing up in New Orleans and surviving Katrina. He told me of younger days in a biker gang and presently bulging hernias. Gnarled fingers grew out of his knotted hands like the branches of an old cypress tree. They were attached to frozen wrists where the bones had fused together.

"I've got rubatide arthritis. Had it for 10 years, now." His pronunciation of the ailment brought serious questions to mind. How could someone live with such inconvenience? How did he deal with the pain? How did he have a disease for 10 years and not know how it was pronounced?

He got me a spot selling newspapers one morning with a crew that picked him up. One of the other guys was sick. A van picked us up in the morning and dropped us off at our respective locations. It seemed to be more about putting a few quarters in the pockets of these decrepit liquor hounds than it did about actually making money. The novelty of notably destitute newspaper vendors on the same street corners every morning must have somehow been good for the press. I just couldn't figure out how.

My hands went numb, and everyone who bought a newspaper asked where Ray was. Some people just asked where he was but didn't buy one. It took over four hours to collect seven singles and 13 dollars more in quarters. When I did, I abandoned my post and walked to Taco Bell. A guy tried to sell me a package of stolen razor blade heads at one of the tables but settled to rip me off by a canal on the other side of a chain link fence. He wouldn't shut up about shooting up in the back of his hands. I should have known not to trust him.

Larry moved into my room from Tracy's place, and whatever pomp he projected that first night in Tracy's apartment had withered with his frame. Now he stood on his crutches and stared into the bathroom mirror, shooting thick mixtures of cocaine and heroin into his neck. His once beautifully conditioned and manicured hair had turned into a matted ball of lint exaggerated by his skeletal frame and the purple track marks running down his jugular vein. There were stragglers from up and down Cerrillos who came in and out of my room day and night. A 24-year-old guy we called Popeye stopped by frequently and bragged about kicking in doors and raping women.

Popeye imagined booty lay on the other side of every window and door he saw, and nights he came around saw me trying to climb up the sides of buildings and into windows impossible to reach. He jumped over the counter at Schlotzky's and took a 20 out of the drawer one day and got away with it. Popeye called me *huero* and always said I was stepping on his toes.

One night I stole seven Ativan out of the bottle in Larry's coat pocket while he slept in a pile of trash in the corner. It had been a hard night for me, because I was sick and mostly unable to sleep from a lack of heroin. He sat up and patted his chest to feel for the bottles when he woke up at around 10 and pulled the bottles out. Eleven pills had turned into four while he slept. He looked at me angry and desperate. I said,

"I'm sorry!"

I made empty promises to repay him, but when he demanded proof, I ripped the microwave out of the wall and stuffed it into the red roll-around suitcase. It still had a laminated card from my grandmother's travel agency and my own information from my flight to New Mexico.

"Call Luna! Tell him to bring a dub!" A dub is a twenty-dollar bag.

"What? You think he is going to want that nasty little thing? You've lost it."

"Just call him! I'll deal with him when he gets here!"

Larry called our dealer, and I could tell Luna was trying to confirm that we had money over the phone, but Larry danced around it until Luna agreed to come anyway. I slid my arms into the sleeves of my NASCAR racing jacket and headed across the parking lot with Larry hobbling on crutches. It was a no. 24 Jeff Gordon racing jacket, bright red with blue flames up the sleeves and a bright blue DUPONT logo on the front. My mom had ordered it for me brand-new, to replace the old dirty one she made me throw away in San Francisco. Larry's crutches creaked in the cold across the asphalt. The suitcase rolled behind me and half of the microwave stuck out. The power cord dragged behind.

It had all unraveled.

As if the bright red racing jacket and microwave in my suitcase and the raggedy old man on crutches didn't attract enough attention, the whole crew of that Schlotzky's knew us by name. They always let us wait for Luna in the store out of the cold and even gave us free drinks from the soda fountain.

The manager smiled at us and asked us how we were doing and walked back to the drive-up window. It was not likely that Luna would accept the microwave and not likely that he would give us a ride to hock it for the measly five bucks it would fetch. I jumped over the counter to hit the cash out button on the register. The drawer opened, and I took a couple of $20 bills. An employee screamed at me. The customers hesitated to get up out of their seats.

I handed Larry a 20 and ran through the parking lot behind the Warren Inn. Somehow, I knew to get rid of my red jacket and went to my room from the other side of the building to change my clothes. The sunglasses, headphones, blue Dickies jacket and backwards Kangol cap were enough of a change that when the cops came into the building to look for me, they asked me if I had seen myself running by in a red jacket.

"No, officer, I haven't seen him." I tried to walk down Cerrillos but it was too cold.

I walked to the building next to mine and knocked on the yeast ball's door. A few days before this I had sold him 20 dollars' worth of laundry detergent and watched him put it in his arm while I did the coke he had bought. He knew I had ripped him off, but there was nowhere else to go now. The cops were coming. I knocked again, but there was no response.

When I finally walked back to the room to meet the cops in the hallway, they smashed my face into the wall and handcuffed me. They already had Larry in the back of a squad car with his crutches and the 20 that I gave him. The cops told me they would let me go with a ticket if I could give them back the other 20, but Larry had warrants and was going to jail either way. As bold as it was to jump over the counter and help myself to the money in the cash box, the cops only charged me petty larceny.

Sitting there in handcuffs, I wasn't embarrassed by gawking onlookers or the slowing traffic. At 19 that was who I was, a criminal junkie, and that is what criminal junkies did. They got arrested at 10:30 on a Tuesday morning for being embarrassingly inept at crime and the whole world saw it. The officers talked amongst themselves and said that they wouldn't go into the room to look for the other 20 because of the filth and stench. That sounded about right.

Larry and I spent three days in jail and went to court on Friday. I took my charges and told the judge I had only come to Santa Fe for school. It was a mystery to me how I ended up jumping over the counter at a restaurant and taking money out of the register. He let me go with time served. Carlos picked me up a week later and took me back to Taos to clean up.

Taos

Winter 2005-Fall 2006

They said Taos was still the wild, wild West, and the shotgun blast through the A in Taos in the green Welcome to Taos County, Population 5761 sign let you know it was. My friend Doh-Doh called it La Tierra de la Manana, because what you do today might as well be done tomorrow, and what you do tomorrow might as well be done next week. No one would know the difference.

The oldest generation still spoke more Spanish than English, and conversations with the locals convinced me they descended from Sancho Panza himself. Maybe in the corner of their mother's attic, the conquistador armor of some lanky and fictitious Spaniard collected dust as a forgotten family heirloom. Maybe he was on the plains tilting at windmills still.

I never knew I could feel that way about a place.

Carlos picked me up after the ridiculous events of the last chapter. Remember? Taking my microwave hostage? Getting lost at the Warren Inn? Larry and his crutches? The yeast ball and selling newspapers? And dropped me off at an old hotel in Ranchos de Taos called the Hacienda Inn. It was two stories and badly neglected. The guy working the front desk had red eyes and a million things to do for his meager wages and pauper's room. That next winter, Doh-Doh and I lived there, shooting cocaine and our lives in shambles. Doh-Doh eventually died, but while we lived there, people told us how scheming the owner could be. He couldn't have been kind to his employees. He wasn't to us.

Taos remained a mystery to me, because I had been reclusive that first month while I had been detoxing in the backroom at Carlos's house. I didn't know anyone but him and his family, but now I would get to know Taos well, the people, the culture, the geography. It was mostly populated by the descendants of the Spanish colonizers from 300 years before. They remained separated from the rest of American culture and progress and spoke a unique brand of Spanglish. You only knew the modern era existed when you drove up and down the main drag, full of McDonald's and Burger King and the rest of it, but in El Prado or Llano Quemado on the right day, it looked like it did when the Spanish first colonized it.

It is said that Taos only knew the Depression ever happened because of the newspaper headlines and everyone was already so poor. From October to March snow falls. The ground is covered in mud after that, and the wind rips until June. Summertime sees monsoons dancing on the horizon or splashing into town, and by late July everything is dusty. When fall finally blows back in from wherever it ran away to, men roast sacks of green hatch chili in rotisserie cages over propane burners out front of every grocery store in town.

It is famous for being an artist's colony and where the first few scenes of "Easy Rider" were filmed, and the gorge bridge where Mickey and Mallory cut their hands in "Natural Born Killers" among other things. I knew real people who came to buy some woven baskets from a guy in town 20 years before or whose van broke down 15 years earlier and had lived there ever since. We called it a spiritual vortex. There was so much to know about Taos and plenty of interesting people, but like I said, all I knew at that point was the Taos Inn and having that rash at Carlos's and now the Hacienda Inn.

After a couple of weeks of paying my rent at the hotel, Carlos took me to an old dilapidated restaurant called the Don Quixote, on the property he owned with a lawyer friend of his. We walked to the back of the place and unlocked a gate over and the old door with a window. The insides were damp and leaky in the cold of late winter, but once upon a time it was the hot spot in town and competed with the Taos Inn and Alley Cantina for evening music venues. It had a restaurant, a bar and a few rooms. In its heyday it saw many travelling artists passing through town, some famous and some unknown. Paul Simon is supposed to have stayed there once, but when I knew the place it bared its bones for the world to see; it was like the carcass of a once vibrant fox now silent and dead still, decaying in the bushes. I lived there.

The old restaurant was evidence of times past. She had in her all the stories and lives and nights of laughter and drinking that were now part of Taos' history. I imagined what things looked like for her over the years and how old my parents would have been when she was built. My friend told me when he was 19 how he had been bounced for getting belligerent. He and his friend shot cocaine in the parking lot till the place closed.

When the bouncer came to lock the back door, my friend jumped out of the truck and stomped the guy until he quit moving. My friend crawled on his belly through ditches and bushes to get away and told me the owner of the place used to count his money over a pile of cocaine in the room where I stayed.

I slept on a futon cushion on the floor with a few blankets. No heat. No hot water. No electricity. No work those first couple days at the old Don Quixote and nothing to do, but a few nights into staying there, someone knocked on the back window. Thirteen guys from Chihuahua had instructions from Carlos to come stay there while they worked for him and until they could figure something else out.

Carlos and his business partner had plans to build a bunch of high-end condominiums on the property, and in the morning, we began to demolish the old adobe structures. The Mexicans smoked weed with me on our break. I talked to them in Spanish. There were Juan, Pepe, Paco, Carlos, Ramiro and Moises among others in the boisterous group. We worked together. We drank beer and ate together. We lived together at the Kit Carson Trailer Park, and it was a magical thing for me, a 19-year-old American kid, to be adopted by a band of migrant workers. They loved me and brought me everywhere they went.

When the 13 men broke up into two groups to move into their respective trailers, Juan invited me to live with him and Moises, his father-in-law, Ramiro and some of the others. I took them up on their offer, and things went well until they showed me the cocaine. We rented our trailer from Juan's brother, who also moved big weight for some cartel members back home.

The first time I ever tried their cocaine, we were floating some drywall in Juan's brother's new double-wide, and they laid this dollar bill out on the counter with some cocaine in it. We had been drinking beers, and they used the corner of a plastic card to do bumps. I rolled up my own dollar bill and scraped together a small line, but before I leaned over it to snort it, Juan slapped my shoulder. He said,

"*No, guero! No hagas tanto!*" No white boy, don't do so much!

In a few minutes, I puked out of the front door and stumbled through the sagebrush trembling and confused. The beer got me more than the cocaine, but it was the best stuff I ever tasted. Another hour passed before the small pile disappeared, and Juan's brother asked me if I wanted more. Of course, I did. He came back holding a white trash bag full of the stuff. He had to use both arms to hold it.

From there my relationship with the Mexicans disintegrated. They noticed I was lazy and didn't like to wake up at 5:30 every day like them. I slept on a mattress in the living room and left my dirty socks lying around. Juan fronted me the $80 for rent on numerous occasions, because I always spent my paychecks on coke. He was kind about it, but he was also getting tired of me and my dirty socks. The guys liked to tease me by saying,

"Chupa mi mion, hue! Chupa mi mion, guero!"

After one night of nosebleeds and staring out the windows, I woke up at 8. They had been awake since 6 cooking breakfast and making a racket in the living room where I slept. I stood at the sink crusty and angry, filling a cup of water. Juan to said it to me. It means suck my d*ck. I threw the cup of water in his face, and he got scared.

They left me alone and crying with my red roll-around suitcase in the dirt parking lot of the Kit Carson trailer park. After that I went back to the old Don Quixote. Carlos wasn't happy to have me move back in, but I worked for him on the site in the daytime. The plaza was full of local kids who smoked weed or did Ecstasy at night or on the weekends.

A couple of underage runaway girls lifted a box of cereal and orange juice from the organic grocery store and smoked a bowl with me under a tree. They stank and wore filthy clothes. They asked me if I wanted to hitchhike back out to the Mesa where they lived in a bus, to drink a fifth of liquor they had. It was a place people called Mad Max Territory and seemed more like a fictional dystopian landscape than a real place.

Craterous roads of beige-colored dust crawled through the sagebrush like varicose veins between Two Peaks and Three Peaks mountains on the Mesa. It was an unforgiving terrain settled over the previous two decades by dreadlocked barbarians with chunks of animal bone in their hair. Some wore the heads and limbs of baby dolls on chains around their necks and patchouli oil. The younger ones had names like Toaster, Scrape, Lost or Chaos. Others lived in piles of dirt-packed tires or old Harvester school buses. Many of them fired shots over your head just to say hello and bragged about their packs of vicious dogs. They liked cheap beer and meth and had warrants or something or someone they were hiding from across the country or some sort of mental illness that had banished them there. Their women were scary and primitive like them and swooned in romantic passion at their men's backhands raised to their faces.

I had been out there a few times that summer, once with those two girls. Another time to worship the moon and dance to drums around a fire. The next morning a strange woman with hairy legs and blue moss on her teeth tried to have sex with me after she worked on my energy. I escaped through the sagebrush to some guy's junkyard, and he smoked hash with me.

By noon, a sunburnt and buzz-cut mother of two came to trade some eggs for a two-finger pouch of tobacco. She scowled, the blue-inked tattoo of some ancient hieroglyph scrawled into her forehead. A barefoot child followed dressed in post-apocalyptic rags, and her naked baby brother slobbered and smiled in her arms, straddling her bony hip. I hitchhiked back into town with a guy who had Cake playing in his truck.

Like I said, it was unreal how lawless it was out there, but Carlos talked my parents into buying a cheap acre of it for me. He figured I fit the description of people crazy enough to live out there. This was when I was 19 and he and my parents thought they could prop me up with money and opportunity, but it never worked. They hadn't noticed my brain was rotten yet.

I only saw the acre twice, once before I bought it and the morning after I got drunk with the two runaways. One of their friends lived in a mud hut next to it and met us with an assault rifle. He never said anything to me, but I got the impression he wanted me to leave.

Back in town I worked for Carlos sometimes. I lived in the Don Quixote and smoked weed up at the park or plaza. It was summertime, and I made friends with a guy who called me 1984 because I had the book with me once. The whites of his eyes were the only parts of him not caked in grease and dirt. He drank Milwaukee's Best and joked that he would have to pull his liver around in a red wagon full of ice soon.

I met a potbellied 36-year-old redhead named Becky on the Fourth of July. She took me home. We smoked weed. I heard the story about her kids and their fathers. Her oldest child's dad hanged himself in a holding cell after a DUI, and we listened to his CD collection. Somehow, she ended up with it. Radiohead. Steely Dan. The Talking Heads. She licked my forearm and bit my neck. I smoked a cigarette on the porch when it was over.

Anytime a one-night stand lasts any longer than one night, it gets weird, and it did for us. I found myself at her house as a live-in boyfriend, but boyfriend isn't the right word. Just something like one, because she had sex with anyone who walked through the door. It was new and exciting, and I liked the idea of an open relationship but found no other suitable female with whom I could copulate. Fact is she wasn't a suitable partner either. It was only that I felt obliged and had nothing else to offer. Between her four kids by three different men, living on food stamps and her bi-monthly disappearances to go smoke crack while I took care of the kids, I was looking for something different. The opportunity only had to show itself, and it did.

It came in the form of an intravenous cokehead named Doh-Doh. The first time I saw him he was trying to sleep off the night before at a friend's house where a pound of mushrooms lay like blue alien turds scattered between half-empty bottles of cloudy beer. It was Becky's friend's place, and there was a small crowd there that afternoon.

Doh-Doh lay on the black leather couch. The air sat still and hot. We screamed over the blaring music and blew big hits of pot and cigarette smoke into the living room. It was going on 4 p.m. There was no way he could have been asleep, but since he pretended Becky and the rest of us pretended also.

A little later Doh-Doh woke up and came outside. He didn't address me much except to talk about music and musicians. Then as is quite common in Taos, horoscopes and astrology came up, because a thick artery of New Age mysticism and so-called spirituality runs through Taos, especially through the white people, who are never more than one generation into being a Taoseno anyway. Real Taosenos don't care about your sign unless it's going to help them get laid. They read my horoscope and I pretended that I cared.

We all sat on plastic lawn chairs and swigged on our beers sweating in the sun. We rubbed our bare feet in the tan-colored dirt and gravel that was supposed to pass for a front yard. From time to time a glass bowl passed among us slowly and lazily under tattered party banners of different colors and lines of broken Christmas lights strewn in a zigzag pattern between the trees. Taos fit me well. The sun's beams still beat down, but not like before. Late afternoon lay over us and took hold of the day. It was the end of summer.

Taos

Winter 2006

Whether the odds were ever stacked against me or not, I don't know. I was against myself. The odds were irrelevant.

Doh-Doh had lost his whole life to cocaine over the 18 months prior to our meeting. Everyone in town knew him as a crackerjack accountant and commercial pot grower with a huge heart. He quit rambling a decade before we met to raise his family. His father strangled his mother and got away with it back in Tennessee; at least that's what he said. He ran away and reinvented himself as a Rainbow kid, eventually becoming an elder. People had been proud of him for finally getting his dentures, but he broke one of the front teeth off while trying to make a tooter out of a pen a few weeks after he got them. Becky and I had plans with him to get a gram of LSD and sell it but it never happened.

He showed me an old picture of himself before he ever tried cocaine. At least 100 pounds had come off him by the time I met him, and his dreadlocks touched the ground in the photo. He cut them off two years earlier in a custody battle for his kids, which he won, but his new girlfriend came home from work one night with a bag of cocaine. He pulled all the money out of his wallet and told her to buy as much as she could after the first line he ever did. It was all gone now, the kids and everything else.

We lived together at Becky's until she kicked him out for accidentally giving her 3-year-old daughter a burnt crack spoon to eat her Fruit Loops. Not to mention his first week of living there, when he and I took Becky's newest boy toy out on an all-night coke binge and left her with the kids at the house. Doh-Doh missed a vein that night and got an abscess, which he drained a few days later with a knife that he bought at Walmart, after drinking a fifth of tequila. Three of her kids watched him cut it open and squeeze the puss into the kitchen sink before he fell on his mattress in the living room. He cried and punched the wall.

When she kicked him out I left, too. We moved to the Hacienda Inn a few doors down from where I detoxed after Carlos brought me back from Santa Fe. We worked every day doing construction and shot up lots of cocaine every night in room 306.

On several occasions our own bad choices reduced us to eating packets of powdered creamer and sugar. We licked the granules from our greasy palms and smacked our tongues to the roofs of our mouths, desperate for sustenance. Doh-Doh had a good point when he said they tasted better together. On the job site another worker got mad at me for eating a loaf of soggy bread he had left there a week before. Our clothes were less like fabric and more like some strange moss that grew on our bodies always damp and cold. When I smoked I tapped cigarette ashes onto my pants and rubbed them in.

Doh-Doh did big shots of cocaine and stared at the curtains and held the syringe in his hand, cupping both of his ears. Blood ran down his arms. His dentures hung halfway out of his mouth. There was no response to anything I said. When I would hallucinate hearing the boots of the SWAT team running up the old iron stairs to bust us, I flushed our stash, and another time I keistered it and walked miles to Becky's house at 3 a.m. to watch "Forrest Gump" until I came down. Doh-Doh said it was a very rude thing to do.

I told you before that the owner of the Hacienda Inn wasn't kind to me and Doh-Doh, and while that may be true, we were not innocent in our dealings with him. For a month or more, we flushed syringe after syringe down the toilet, until it finally backed up. Water leaked through the ceiling into the room below us, and the owner kicked us out the next day. He tried to keep our stuff, but the disgruntled employees let us grab what we could. It wasn't like we had anything valuable.

Carlos had just purchased a 1994 blue Chevy S10 for me with money my parents sent him. We put the truck in my name, and Doh-Doh found me the next day. It was around Thanksgiving, and our friends, a lesbian couple with a baby, let us stay at their place for the week while they visited family in Portales. We did big shots of cocaine like always, and I almost burned the building down, afraid of the shadow people.

Doh-Doh talked me into jumping through the neighbor's window and borrowing the DVD player and flat screen without ever talking to the guy. Doh-Doh said it was cool, because he had done a mutual friend's taxes once. I don't think we ever watched a movie, but when the neighbor, his girlfriend and the landlord busted through the door, we had rags over our mouths and the room smelled like paint thinner. I can't remember what we said, but it's hard to imagine our words were any consolation to the incensed trio. The girl accused me of being a peeping tom. It was not clear how she got that idea, but the stolen electronics in our possession and the solvent-soaked rag in my hand made me feel like I wasn't credible. I kept quiet.

The lesbian couple and their baby got kicked out because of our antics. We moved into another hotel in town called the Indian Hills, into room 234. Directly above our room, the super intendant lived. He was a Vietnam vet and had run with the Hell's Angels. Half of the "bone" structure in his face was reshaped X-ray film, replacing the bone eaten by a benign tumor he had in his 20s. He could snort a whole bag of cocaine, plastic and all, into his sinus cavities for storage purposes and cough it up later. One night, he took my hand and shoved my pinky up his nose so I could feel the cavern. We smoked crack with him, sometimes, but Doh-Doh and I continued to shoot up large quantities of cocaine every chance we got.

Work dried up for us by the end of December, and my parents paid for a plane ticket back home. In the week I spent there, I stole money, smoked crack and found out I had Hepatitis C. When they sent me back to New Mexico, I bought some crack from a guy who stole my wallet in Albuquerque. It had $500 in it. In Santa Fe I rented the truck out to a crack dealer for a $20 rock.

The truck never came back. I sat in the back room of an angry crackhead's apartment for days watching "Gangs of New York" and feeling sick. He had enough of me being there one day and dropped me off on the Interstate in a snow storm to hitchhike back up to Taos.

Sometime after getting back to Taos I lived in a house on Montoya Street that Carlos owned. He gave me a job. I found a puppy that needed a home, and since I couldn't take care of myself, I adopted her. She covered the back room of the house on Montoya with lumpy Tootsie rolls and silver-dollar puddles of pee while I went to work and smoked crack at the Indian Hills Hotel with Doh-Doh on the weekends.

Carlos had a friend who was a shaman. The guy wanted to help me with a medicine called yopo, the intensely unpleasant and hallucinogenic snuff of an ancient indigenous bean. He told me it would change my life. He told me I would vomit. He told me to fast from food 24 hours before we took it. I smoked hundreds of dollars' worth of crack with Doh-Doh the night before instead.

When it was time to take the medicine and have ceremony with Gustavo, the shaman, I was nowhere to be found. They called, but I never answered.

On Sunday evening, they found me and talked to me in Carlos's car.

"So I want to help you, Riley, but now that you disappeared like this I'm concerned. I have to see that you are serious." Gustavo spoke English well.

"I understand. I want help too. It's not like I want to keep living like this, but I can't stop."

"Okay. Well, I talked to Carlos, and what I want to see is you live in the jungle with a tribe called the Shipibo tribe. The jungle is very hard to live in. You have to know that. Even I wouldn't want to live there, but I want you to live there for at least three months. It will help me see that you are serious. Besides, they can do a lot of good for you. They specialize in a medicine called ayahuasca."

Carlos talked to my parents and set up a date in early February when I would go down to Peru. While I waited to leave Taos two of Carlos's friends came to visit and film for a movie they planned to make about Gustavo that weekend. A 28-year-old Tulane University graduate who lived in Uptown New Orleans produced the piece. His name was Jerry, and a 6'8" black Cuban man named Timothy had the camera. They wanted to make a documentary about Gustavo and the oppressed native culture down in South America. Carlos asked me if I would give an honest record of my drug abuse and life on the streets for the camera. My confessions on camera changed the emotional tone of the room, but I said crazy things like,

"I mean. Yeah. I slept on the streets. I ate out of trashcans. But at least I brushed my teeth every day." That didn't make sense, and it wasn't true anyway.

I did coke with Doh-Doh a few more times and tripped acid with him one weekend, but the last time I saw him he was walking down Montoya to where he was staying with a girl. It was at sunset, and he walked in defeated posture. My puppy chased him down the road a bit before he brought her back. We didn't say much other than that we would see each other again. Our days of being road dogs had come to an end. He died shortly after that.

Doh-Doh talked bad about his buddy's wife one day. His friend beat him up and kicked him in the head. He got on a plane to Hawaii, where he intended to start over. His brain hemorrhaged from the altitude of the flight, and Doh-Doh never woke up in the islands.

It was beginning to seem like everywhere I went things went bad. The people I hung out with hurt and acted crazy and shot big amounts of drugs and destroyed everything they touched. I was the same as them, so everywhere I went that's what I found. Now I had plans to move to the jungle of Peru to live with witch doctors, which sounded crazy, but it might be crazy enough to work.

Peru

Winter 2007- Fall 2008

Carlos arranged for the guys making the movie to accompany me to Peru, and we stayed at Gustavo's hotel in Pisac. Jerry planned to make the movie about Gustavo's community, but Timothy decided that my stories of addiction and the dynamic of trying to change my life in the jungle with the Shipibo tribe was more viable and certainly more interesting than whatever they had planned with Gustavo. It was a funny thing for them to choose me because they only came with me to make sure I didn't disappear on a coke binge before I got to the jungle.

Timothy and I got along great, but I didn't like Jerry. He was privileged, white and from the South. I hated these things about myself and didn't like them in him either. Not that I made special effort to like people back then. If you've read the things I've written so far, it's not hard to tell how difficult and unfriendly I could be, but they decided to make their movie about me after Jerry gave in to Timothy's prodding. They called it "A Crooked Line" and would spend hundreds of thousands of dollars over four years to document absolutely no change in me.

Gustavo took us to different places around the area and taught us about the Andean culture. It was a profound experience for all of us to learn about the beautiful way of life destroyed by Spanish colonization and the Catholic Church centuries before. In our down time at the hotel, I used my Spanish to be sweet to one of the girls who worked there, but when I asked her for a date she turned me down, having some long-standing and rocky relationship in the way.

The natives cover their faces when photos are taken as a rejection of their individuality, because they are nothing by themselves. Instead of handshakes, they greet each other by grabbing each other's wrists, signifying the reciprocity that exists in their culture. There is no word for thank you or sorry because those are actions, not words. Gustavo also taught us how they moved those huge stones and built the megaliths that became the ruins we were visiting.

Each stone is unique from any other, but they all fit together so that not a sheet of paper can be put between them centuries later. One stone was assigned to one family that worked closely with the families making the stones surrounding theirs. Different families and individuals worked closely with other families or individuals to create a strong community. Like the unique stones working in harmony to create an indestructible form without mortar.

Shamanism and folklore laid the foundations of their culture. Celebrations and customs and their dress were all based on the seasons and the cultivation of crops. Nature meant everything to them, and they were never alone, because the rocks, hills, trees and everything else lived and breathed in harmonious existence with them.

I was a product of Western civilization and extremely privileged but entitled, addicted and angry. Here, this culture had nothing I had growing up, but they were content. Despite all they suffered, they smiled and knew how to live. I had everything but wanted to die. Gustavo believed that the introspection obtained through shamanic medicines and immersion in a culture built on community and nature would help me overcome drugs.

He explained how rats isolated in cages choose cocaine over food and water till they die, but rats that live in a community and have quality of life choose to live by eating and drinking when cocaine is available. I saw his point. My cold, internal isolation was responsible for at least some of what was wrong, and I had nothing to lose. The sound man and cameraman from the movie crew flew to Pucallpa with me and the Shipibo shaman who would attempt to heal me of my addiction. His name was Teo Valdo.

I knew things were different the second the hot humid air pushed through the doorway of the plane and I walked down onto the tarmac. It was like movies I had seen as a kid about Vietnam, and droves of modified dirt bikes with three wheels and a carriage for passengers called mototaxis filled the atmosphere with the chorus of their two-stroke drone. Everyone wore flip-flops and their open personalities matched their scant clothing. They talked in a distinct jungle dialect of Spanish. The dirt bike rickshaws buzzed through town on roads of red clay and carried as many as seven people at a time and maybe some live chickens tied upside down, a bushel of plantains or a squealing pig.

Teo Valdo took us to the hotel where we spent the night and came back in the morning to take us to the river port. We walked four blocks to the port market. It teemed with commerce and activity. Barefoot men carried large quantities of plantains on their backs and grunted up the muddy bank of the river and loaded them into trucks. From small canoes, women and children sold bags of bread or apples or rice and chicken meals wrapped in banana leaves to passengers waiting on the boats for departure to their village. Frantic crowds of men and women jumped up and down and bargained over the pigs or chickens or bags of grain poor families of farmers had brought into town earlier that morning.

We maneuvered up a plank from the mud into a wooden boat; we ducked our heads under the roof and crawled over other passengers to our seats at the middle of the boat. A light drizzle started. It was clear that we were in a different world, and whatever I thought mattered back in America didn't matter here.

We waited more than an hour to take off and when we finally did it was slow. It took six hours to get there, so we talked to a small group of Americans coming out to the Shipibo village with us. They had met Teo Valdo some months earlier and wanted to visit his wife's family's village, Ceylan, and they were coming with us.

Our clothes stuck to our skin, and our backs cramped on the tiny wooden seat before we arrived. Red clay stuck to our shoes as we got off the boat, and a group of women halfway danced in traditional Shipibo garb. The men played clumsy drums and flutes to greet us. A hoard of kids carried our bags a half mile up to the hut where we would sleep and invited us to eat chicken and dance in a different hut by an enormous puddle they called the soccer field.

My lungs struggled to breathe the soggy air, and mosquitos bit our skin through the repellent. It was hot and still and muddy and arguably the most miserable place I had ever been in my life. No matter how cool it sounded to live in the jungle, it wasn't. We only escaped the mosquitos under our nets, but the air sat stiller and hotter under them. Different bugs or biting ants usually made their way into the damp bedding.

The whole boat ride into the jungle the other Americans with us boasted how they would fast for several days in preparation for the ayahuasca ceremonies and they had big plans to stay for a week or more and do several ceremonies. But the women left less than 24 hours in and the men only made it another 12 before they took off after the first ceremony. Throughout my time in the jungle, Canadians, Americans and Europeans alike would come with big ambitions about how long they would stay and tell me how happy they were to be there, but when the mosquitoes became reality and heat beat them down and ants were crawling in their beds, they always left frazzled and desperate for a porcelain toilet and air conditioning. Me on the other hand, I didn't have a choice. The jungle days in a tribal village were the life I was living at the time. There wasn't anywhere else for me to go.

But we had ceremony the first night, before that first group of Americans left. It was with Teo and his wife, Marina, and her whole family: her mother and father, three brothers and their wives, two of her sisters, besides cousins and uncles and aunts, maybe 25 people. We sat in a circle and took turns letting the alkaline sludge slide down our throats before Teo blew out the kerosene lamp and lit a cigarette. Mosquitos bit every part of us. He began ceremony with a guttural moaning that ascended into a chorus of him and his in-laws singing slithering incantations to the snake spirit. Teo fanned random members of our party with a large eagle feather and sang songs particular to that individual. He put his mouth to each one's head and sucked loudly before puking into a bucket. A cousin stood and sang loudly. He made strange geometrical patterns in the dark with his cigarette.

The jungle swallowed my mind, and the entomological chirps of the life teeming all around coursed through my veins. I could feel the silent vegetation encroaching and knew it could make me disappear in a second like a scene from "Jumanji." The spirit spoke to us each in our own way, and we shared our experiences through the broken Spanish of one of the other visitors before we all crawled under our mosquito nets and slept.

The guys from the movie interviewed me in the morning sitting around a smoldering fire with one of the cousins and his friend cooking up the next batch of ayahuasca in a big pot. I talked about my hepatitis and what I thought about the medicines curing it. It was hard to imagine that there was much Teo could do for me with ayahuasca and the other plants. We talked about this and that on camera before they hugged me and took off to catch a boat into the city. They would be back in a few months to get more footage and catch up with me.

Besides ceremony there was nothing to do but read, and the days passed slow and hot. I got diarrhea from the microbes in the well water. It was so bad that I cried in the outhouse. Teo's family adopted me as their own. They called me "Bebe Grande" on account of all the candy I ate, and I was very close to their youngest, Brian. He was only 2 and loved to eat bananas.

Once a month or so they would bring me back into their house in Pucallpa, where their other six kids lived and went to school. It was a tiny wooden house with a corrugated tin roof, and as many as 19 people slept on the floor in a night. I imagined the tin roof would glow like a coil in the oven from all the radiation it had soaked up during the daytime, but it never did. An outhouse sat about 10 feet from the back door, and when the back yard flooded from the rain, water licked the threshold. I spent as much time as possible at phone parlors called locutorios and used the computers to watch YouTube videos or read Wikipedia articles and use Facebook. Sometimes I called the girl working at Gustavo's hotel to tell her that I loved her.

We never stayed in the city more than a few days before we returned by boat to Ceylan, where we cooked everything on open fires and the roofs were made of neatly folded palm fronds instead of corrugated tin and the mosquitoes bit. There were different boats, but we always got on the one going to Masisea, which was a tiny century-old settlement where something like 2,000 people lived. It was two miles up a dirt road from where we lived in Ceylan, and a pharmacy and a barbershop sat on one side of the plaza. On the other side were several stores selling butchered chicken out of a bucket, hot bottles of soda, crackers, cookies, clothes, and instant coffee with fried eggs and rice for a lunch-time meal. A couple of bars ran big speakers and refrigerators on generators at night while people danced and drank beer at tables. At a few small, covered stations along the road, men and women sold gasoline out of plastic jugs and poured it into motorcycle tanks through funnels with cloth filters. I visited from time to time, but it wasn't much to see. One of Marina's sisters had a little store in the village that sold cigarettes and candy, which was all I ever bought anyway.

We continued with the shamanic treatments at night, and sometimes ceremony would shake me to the core. On one occasion I had no recollection of coming up into "the plateau" or anything other than a thick fog rolling over me before it transported my whole body, not my mind or imagination but my physical body.

In the vision I was in a similar village, where men in tactical gear burned huts to the ground with flamethrowers. The men slaughtered Asian-looking adults and collected the children in cages to be carried away to some horrific fate, but I wasn't sure where. Whatever was happening wasn't clear to me, but I knew that it was a reality for someone somewhere at some time. The terror of it poured through my veins like acid. I woke up from it completely sober and troubled by the vision. Teo Valdo told me that the medicine had a conscience and could impart knowledge or healing at her own will. What I saw was the reality of human trafficking, and it scared me.

Another time an American girl who came to stay with us told me in the middle of ceremony that a fairy was stroking her hair and telling her that she was beautiful. She laughed and said that she was being healed of her poor self-image and deep hurts in her life by the love and affirmation of the fairy. She laughed harder and said that the fairy was pulling her hair now and that it was getting to be too much. Before it was over a strange, chirping language that was not human seemed to be channeled through her and stifled her terrified screams. She sounded like a fairy, and the memory has never left me. In that same ceremony I felt sick but couldn't puke. Teo sang over me and fanned me with his eagle feather, and I purged immediately. I almost never puked. Teo sang again, and the sound and letters a strange digital language washed over me. The medicine reacted to the influence he exerted over it.

I thought a lot about different things to get through the boredom of months in the jungle. I imagined the large dirt hives of termites to be piles of cocaine and thought about starting a grow operation back in the States when I returned. The Shipibo language fascinated me, and I thought about it.

Shipibo makes phonetic distinctions between words that originate in the lower throat or are created by movements of the tongue and lips not used in English. It was a chipper language and guttural and primal, with the Spanish alphabet crudely representing it on paper. I imagined the language had evolved in the jungle bush and ants had carried it off the branches into the minds of the natives through their ears. It seemed to mimic mating rituals between wild birds or monkeys in the trees. The hoots of nocturnal birds and croaks of lazy frogs have contributed to the Shipibo vocabulary. I wanted to speak it so badly but couldn't get much further than words for scrambled eggs, fried plantains, good morning, hurry and you are pretty.

My father sent me big boxes of books to pass the time. I read James Joyce, Steinbeck, as much of Kurt Vonnegut as I could, Tom Robbins and everything else. I read an 800-page biography on Che Guevara and idolized his socialist ideology and devotion to the cause. He probably would have killed me for being a lazy, white, drug-addicted American, but that didn't matter to me. When I read that people were upset at the executions he oversaw after the Revolution, I didn't understand. Deep down, I knew that no one's life had any more inherent value than the fish or bacteria from which it evolved, so why would executions offend me?

Our greatest purpose was to die as transitional forms, evolving to perfect the species. I wondered if some future museum might display a life-sized replica of me in my habitat, like we have for cavemen today. It would be made of fiberglass and plaster mold. My dwelling would be behind a dumpster. My shoes would be wet, and instead of prehistoric tools, there would be a lighter and a spoon in my hands, a dirty syringe behind my ear. I would represent a failed branch of the evolutionary process, a glitch in mutation that expressed a fatal trait: Auto-Cerebral Cannibalism. Luckily only the fit survive, and I wasn't it.

Auto-Cerebral Cannibalism. I imagined myself sitting at a table and spooning up my own brain like a melon, but that did not adequately convey the inner horror. The grainy visual of my own brain somehow eating itself was getting closer, but the image of my brain devouring me from the legs up with all the bloodiness and ferocity of an oversized piranha was the only image that seemed sufficiently heinous to me. The thoughts and beliefs in my own mind were destroying me. Even though I didn't know how they got there or what they were, they vehemently and violently opposed me. At least part of it was that I hated myself for being white, male, educated and American. You see? I rejected my father and all that he was, but you can't reject your father without rejecting yourself. So, I did, and it would kill me. That was okay though. It would be a favor to the world.

In the three months we did something like 30 ayahuasca ceremonies, and when it was over Carlos came with the guys making the movie to take me back to Pisac. We had a big celebration and danced all night with the Shipibos before we left in the morning, and I loved the hot shower and sit on porcelain at the hotel.

My mom met us in Pisac and did some interviews with us, and before they all left it was decided that I would live and work for Gustavo in Pisac for the next 10 months. The girl who worked for him had me interested enough so I didn't make much fuss about staying.

I enjoyed talking to tourists who came into Gustavo's restaurant and hotel. The American boy living abroad and immersed in a culture and language they could only experience briefly infatuated them. I told them about my past and that Gustavo believing in me was a catalyst to my turnaround in Peru. It seemed like things would change for the first time in my life.

But my sister came to visit for my birthday, and when she got to town we had lunch and cake that I could barely eat at the hotel. That night we had some beers with the girls from work, when one of them pointed out a white crust hanging out of my nose. Nosebleeds started soon after that, but my sister pretended that everything was okay anyway.

While she was in town I took her to visit different sites of ancient ruins, but it was difficult to take the long walks up and down the old terra forms. I always needed another line and left her hanging in awkward situations while I chased a bag through the cobblestone streets or did coke in the bathroom. When I came back my stories had holes, and I sweated and sniffled and labored to breathe. I got paranoid and demanded that the girl who worked at the hotel with me admit her boyfriend planned to kill me. My sister's last 30 bucks disappeared before she left in a cab.

The bender lasted another few days before Gustavo confronted me by the gate in the wall around his house. He was stern, and when I punched the wall he pushed his forehead into mine and walked me backwards. I told him three times to get out of my face before I punched him. The sequence of events is hazy after that.

I pulled my pocketknife out and stuck it in my stomach in front of everyone in the plaza and chased him toward his front door. He fell, and I broke a heavy potted plant on his leg. At some point I lifted the knife toward my left ear, where I planned to bury it in my neck and pull it across. His gardener grabbed the knife out of my hand and threw it over the wall. Gustavo's 3-year-old son watched the whole thing happen.

I walked back to the hotel somehow and gathered my clothes before I fell on the ground in front of Gustavo's patrons as if the small stab wound was causing me to bleed out. Gustavo threw his hands in the air and complained to the girls who worked there. The next thing I knew I was in one of the hotel rooms with a nurse who would help me get to sleep. She gave me an IV shot of Valium for being ridiculous, and when I woke up the same nurse gave me a shot in the butt cheek this time. My father would have to come get me.

When my dad showed up, we got along great considering all I had pulled and that he was only there to help me get back to the jungle. Since I didn't give him any real trouble right off the bat he assumed the best. We went to drink beer and talked about different things that we both liked, but that night I stole money from him while he slept, and took a taxi to Cusco.

Teo and Marina had come to help him, and we planned to take a bus from Cusco to Pucallpa. Outside of the bus station I told my dad that I left my hat at one of the bars by the plaza and needed to get it.

"Well. You're going to have to go without it. I'll get you another one."

When he turned around for a second, I jumped into a cab and took off. I spent all the money I had on a bag of fake cocaine. It was so frustrating that I sat down on some dirty stairs and held my sweaty head in my hands until my dad came with one of the other girls from the hotel. I refused to leave until I had some cocaine and forced him to buy me a bag in exchange for my cooperation.

Teo and Marina had already taken the bus to Pucallpa, but my dad and I would wait for a plane ticket in a couple of days. He was too embarrassed to return to Pisac, so we went to another little town to wait. In front of my dad and the taxi driver, I blatantly solicited the girl who had helped him find me for sex, which she rejected. We got a hotel, and my father divvied the cocaine up into small paper bindles, which he used to control my behavior.

Gustavo's gardener visited us a few times, and one afternoon my dad and I drank beer in a crumbling hole of a bar with a dirt floor. I demanded a younger patron explain to me how he lost his eye even though it humiliated him. My dad told me to drop it, and I raised my voice. At night, I walked streets of black stone hoping to find trouble. And I did when someone outside of a bar asked me,

"Hey, Gringo, do you want to knife fight?"

"Yes. With you? Where are the knives?"

I was calling his bluff as much as anything. He yelled to one of his buddies by the bar to go get so and so and bring the knives. I stared down at my feet in wet gravel and scattered trash. All I could think about were my own blood-soaked socks and the despair of my father walking up to the scene if my throat were slashed. It was everything I ever wanted.

"What's taking so long? Didn't you ask me if I wanted to knife fight?" He pretended not to hear me, and I walked away.

I bought blister packets of Xanax and harangued my father day and night while he tried to keep me calm between doling out the tiny bindles of coke. When we got to Pucallpa, he had to hire a police officer to keep me from hurting him or myself until the next morning, when we met Teo and Marina at the port. He said he would see me in two months, and I got on a boat in the rain with Teo and Marina.

I was back in the jungle with the Shipibos depressed and hating my life. Two months turned into three. Three months turned into four. Four months turned into five, and month after month passed with no kind of plan to come home or do anything different.

The jungle became my home, whether the city of Pucallpa or the village of Ceylan. It was where I lived, and everyone knew me. I had considered the popular music in Peru to be garbage when I first arrived, but as time went on I came to love the cumbia groups like Mallanep, Kaliente de Iquitos, Papillon, and the rest of them that made speakers sweat sex and demand your body bounce to the beat. Even when I went to the internet cafes by the house in Pucallpa, I listened to the local groups instead of American music. When Marina and the kids watched TV at the house, I watched the variety and comedy shows like them.

Marina loved me like her own kid. She could say things that would annoy me like any mother can, but I loved her very much. We were close. I wish I could say the same about Teo, but it wasn't like that. He showed great patience with me and my antics, but I could not stand communicating with him. His voice and the way he spoke Spanish made me angry. It was partly his need to give an answer to things he didn't understand (exacerbated by the attention and adoration he received from foreigners). The kids all loved me. Luz was 4 and laughed at me but wouldn't hug me. Brian always wanted a bite of my food and called me "amiguito." The other kids all liked me too, except the second oldest daughter. She thought I was rude, and she was right.

I don't know the things that go through a Shipibo's head, and they didn't know what went through my head either. The differences in our cultures were immense. Most of the kids living in the village with me didn't speak Spanish until they were 11. They walked around barefoot and excitedly ate the burnt, black rice out of cooking pots as a snack. Their mothers washed all their clothes by hand. Their fathers caught their dinner daily, and if they had work, the most they could hope to earn was a dollar or two for the day. Many of those women had never seen a sanitary napkin or taken a hot shower. The only prescription for an abscessed tooth was to hold your hand on your cheek until it went away, but the life they lived produced the gentlest and kindest human beings.

Marina's oldest sister, Soila, wins the prize for most amazing person I have ever met. She spoke soft and sweet and probably still has a kid every three years with her husband who looks 15 years younger than she does. Her eyes were always red, and she spent her days tending to the fire, carrying water, sweeping the floor and holding her baby like any other Shipiba in the village. I doubt if she can think poorly of someone.

These weren't the brown faces of strangers in an airport parking lot or the family in worn sandals and hand-stitched clothing selling toys made of wood and string at some tourist trap. These were my brothers and sisters, my aunts and uncles, my mother and father, my grandparents. This was my family.

We carried water in buckets from the wells back to the huts together and swatted at our legs and backs with a towel every evening to keep mosquitoes from biting us. We all slept on the floor with a small mat under nets and trudged through the mud in our flip-flops when it rained. We ate mangos when they fell out of the trees and bore banana bushels or sacks of papayas on our backs from where they grew by the river. Sometimes we walked miles at 3 a.m. to catch a boat back into the city and shared our seats with squealing pigs or clucking chickens. It was not a temporary state of affairs for them, but an unchanging reality. Hot showers, epidurals, Albertson's and air conditioning were things they did not know and probably never would.

After I had been in Peru for about nine months, Timothy came to visit me in the jungle for a couple of weeks before my dad came a second time. He and I talked to various locals about life around there, the drug trade and what they thought about me. A young man named Carlos sold flip-flops out of a big bag he carried on his shoulder along the dirt road between Masisea and our village. He came with two young girls who wanted to meet me, and he told me about Jesus Christ. I quickly shot him down and told him he betrayed his indigenous heritage with his faith.

"Christians killed your ancestors and destroyed their culture hundreds of years ago. Then they gave the survivors new names before they used them as slaves to build their empire. Don't you understand?"

Sometime later the cameraman and I found Carlos organizing a small worship event in the plaza of Masisea. We sat on wooden benches in the dirt. A girl wept and held her open hands high in the air. I asked him,

"Why is she crying? Why are people crying about this? I don't get it!"

"Because of their faith, Riley. Because of their faith."

I found the idea of faith in an invisible man who never existed in the first place to be revolting. Carlos didn't waver in his statement or look for my approval. He stated it as the fact that it was to him, and suddenly I recalled sitting in an ice cream parlor with my mother's father, Turkey.

"Riley, do you pray to God?" Turkey asked. Problems had been a part of my life for years by then. I smoked weed and cigarettes every day and had already talked to three different counselors.

"God? What do you mean God? What in the hell has he ever done for me?"

"I don't know, Riley. Only you and God can know that."

When my father showed up, we slept in the same hotel room in Pucallpa, and I stole a bunch of change out of his shoe in the morning. It had been four months since I did any cocaine, but I found out the shoe shiners outside of the hotel could get grams for $7.

On the boat in, he knew I was high and accused me of it before we got to the village. There was a big celebration for his arrival with dancing and music and food and some beer. I screamed and punched him till Marina's brothers pulled me off him. The night went on, and the party transitioned from dancing and celebrating to careful gazing at the lunatic and his father having it out. Cumbia still blared, but the dancing stopped sometime after I started getting violent.

I sat cross-legged, hunched over in a pair of cargo shorts on the floor. Somewhere, a generator hummed, powering the light bulb hanging over my head and speakers outside. My father stood on the other side of the huts small walls and looked at me through the mesh screen. It was turning into one of the kind of nights only I could give him. Somehow, I had gotten a hold of a black-handled paring knife with a 5-inch blade, and I screamed at him. Strands of slobber fluttered in the jets of air shooting from between my teeth as I convinced him and myself that it was his fault. He was to blame for the way I was and why I wanted to hurt myself. My conviction was an act, but I told him plainly that I hated him. I buried the blade to the hilt three times in the meat of my right calf before I chucked the knife end over end at his face.

I think the problem for us was that we were too much alike, and I think he would agree that he saw things in me growing up that he hated in himself. There were good things too, but I mostly remembered the bad.

I peed on him once, when he changed my diaper. It was on purpose and made me laugh. He swatted at the golden arc of liquid with his hand and griped.

"C'mon, Riley. Don't do that, baby!" Usually, people are impressed I can remember back to when he changed my diapers.

I always say it's easy to remember, because I was 16 when it happened. That's a joke.

On a trip to Mexico once, my father pulled me into the bathroom and very seriously said,

"Riley, I am going to share something very important with you. It's something the Chapman men all know how to do, and you will, too." I was excited and nervous about the family secret he was about to reveal to me. I wondered what it could be. What piece of my identity as a male in our family would he reveal to me? What knowledge would he impart? What honor? What prestige? "This is important. My father taught me. His father taught him, and now, I am going to teach you."

He looked in the mirror, leaned in close to it and pushed the tip of his nose up, before revealing scissors in his other hand. The discourse began, "When you trim your nose hair, you want to . . ."

He taught me how to read on his lap every night after he got off work. School failed to teach me because I skipped pre-K and started kindergarten at the very end of the year. It took a lot of time and effort, but I owe 100 percent of that to him.

He checked my math homework every morning in middle school, and when I got four wrong, he would berate me at the kitchen table in front of my sisters until he took us to school. I can't remember if I cried.

He left me in the jungle after a couple of days, but before he did, he asked me to show him my leg where I stabbed myself. We hadn't talked since that night. He told me to keep them open and breathing and that the wounds would probably be fine if I did, but,

"If there's any problem, call me. I'll tell you what to get." The whole point of his visit was to determine if I was ready to come home or not, and it was clear that I was not.

After that, I would leave the village at night and walk the dirt road up to Masisea to drink homemade wine with whomever I found and smoke pasta basuco. Pasta basuco is the crude extract from the production of real cocaine. It's poisonous and is essentially waste, but it is a freebase cocaine that can be smoked. The price is very cheap. Basuco may come from the similar Spanish word basura for trash because it is refuse from the production of higher quality product. But basuco is also the word for bazooka, possibly referring to the intensity of the high. Like the crack epidemic of the 1980s in big U.S. cities, so pasta is big in South America. Smoking it was a last resort for me, but it happened from time to time.

    To smoke it you roll a quarter of the tobacco out of a cigarette and suck the powder from the tiny bindle of pasta into the cigarette. Once it is all sucked up, you roll the cigarette pointing up between your hands and then grab it by the loose end to swing it back and forth to pack the tobacco and pasta powder together. After that you twist close the loose end and pull the cotton out of the filter to replace it with broken matchsticks. It's ready to go at that point. They sold for about 30 cents apiece, and one was enough to make a man puke.

    I bought the pasta in Masisea from a gay teenager, and I smoked them in the back room of his jungle shack. While I made up the cigarettes to smoke, he would unzip me and pull me out of my pants. I would push his head off me, zip my pants up and button them. Once I lit the cigarette and began to smoke the drugs, he would unbutton and unzip me again and lick my torso, and 15 seconds later when the drugs were all smoked up, I would push him off me. We went through it over and over until all 11 bindles were smoked up.

After smoking all night in Masisea, I would walk on the dirt road crawling with bullet ants and snakes back to the village. Marina's parents and everyone else in the village knew I was smoking drugs, and they made plans to send me back to Pucallpa, where Teo was with his family (probably hiding out from having to deal with me). At the house in Pucallpa, the kids caught me rolling up some pasta into a cigarette, and I smoked it in the outhouse. Teo Valdo got mad. It was the only time I ever saw him like that.

I continued to smoke pasta in Pucallpa and borrowed money from the neighbors to do it. A guy who lived around the corner loaned me money and took me on his mototaxi to a place called Paradise to buy it. He parked far away and made me walk, because it was so dangerous. Teo and Marina would send one the kids to follow me to the graveyards, where I spent my time and smoked pasta. Marina cried over it.

Eventually everyone got tired of it (me most of all), and I asked my mom to help me visit some Americans I knew living in

Tarapoto. My mother believed that I was sober and paid for a ticket. On the bus, a middle-aged woman across the aisle from me moaned in ecstasy and wrapped her hand in the curtains and pushed her head back into the seat in the dark. I knew she wanted me to make a move, so I jumped into the seat next to her and grabbed her thigh.

"What are you doing, Gringo? Go back to your seat! Now!" I had imagined it.

After 16 hours on the bus I woke up in a concrete ditch in Tarapoto with traffic buzzing all around me. The Americans who let me stay with them kicked me out for eating their cereal in the middle of the night. Cheap hotels became my home, and some guys I met showed me how to use a pry bar and a piece of wire to get coins out of the pay phones. I broke a lot of hearts those two months in Tarapoto and snorted a lot of cocaine, of course.

El Callao, Peru
Summer 2008

Getting bludgeoned to death isn't as fun as it sounds. The thought occurred to me as my own brutal death unfolded one night under a street lamp. Most people come to that conclusion without taking things that far, but I never was that kind of person.

To the locals I was a drug-addicted American in a place he didn't belong, doing things he ought not, and getting exactly what he asked for. El Callao is a port well known for its violence. I turned 22 in the three months that I lived there, and no one knew my name. They just called me gringo.

Six men chased me through eight lanes of traffic and I fell twice before they caught me. A pair of work boots and dirty tennis shoes shuffled and twisted for leverage on the pavement in the dim street light between unforgiving cracks of something heavy against the back of my skull. It is a gruesome thought to be beaten to death with rocks. I wanted my mother. I wanted to apologize, but it was over now. Life never flashed before my eyes, only shame as I lost my bowels.

Before I ever moved to El Callao there was a guy in Tarapoto named Luis, who I spent a lot time with. He helped me get my cocaine and went on missions with me to the bar for women, who we usually brought back to my hotel room two at a time. He came to see me off at the airport. I had to keep asking him if I was being set up. There were imaginary men in tactical gear hiding in the airport's bushes that terrified me. I did my last line of cocaine in the bathroom and tried to use the urinal, but my focus was on the window. Police would pour into the bathroom any second and arrest me. An old janitor made sexual advances as I tried to pee, but I wasn't interested and peered over my shoulder.

Luis sipped a beer in the restaurant while I downed a pint bottle of liquor. He assured me there was no ambush coming, but I didn't believe him. It was the last time I saw him, and the last light of dusk faded into night through the airport windows as I walked up to the ticket counter.

"Are you going to be okay to fly, *Senor* Chapman?" The freckly faced girl asked me in Spanish with a look of doubtful concern. Her company uniform and elegant bun made her look smart. I smelled drunk.

"Yes, ma'am."

"So, no problems on the flight?"

"None."

"Very well." Her eyes rolled. She stamped my ticket and directed me to the security checkpoint.

Toward the end of the flight, a lady next to me struck up friendly conversation. She and her sister in the seat next to her lived in Lima and were delighted to know that I was American. I talked and stared indifferently at the light of the city glowing beneath the clouds. Didn't she realize that I smelled like alcohol? The effects of cocaine faded. Her offers for me to stay at her house and meet her family proved that she did not know me or what I was about.

Outside of the airport's automatic sliding doors, the night air was cool on my face, and the cherry of my Caribe cigarette glowed red as I drew in smoke. A blanket of grey clouds sat low over the city buildings. Three hundred *soles* are 100 U.S. dollars, and it was all I had except for my backpack with some notebooks, my passport, and the clothes I wore.

A short, light-skinned man in his black taxi uniform solicited me for a ride, but cocaine and a cheap room close to the airport were all I was interested in, so he pointed me to his slightly fatter workmate. I paid 14 dollars for a couple OF grams and $7 more for a room at Hostal Dax, on Dominicos Avenue and Tomas Valle.

Bustling streets between dilapidated buildings drew me in. El Callao had a peculiar allure. It was real. I identified with its pain. Day-to-day life continued without looking up to acknowledge me as a visitor. There was nothing for gringos there, and no one spoke English. Across Tomas Valle from Hostel Dax, the smoke of cooked animal fat filled the air as women sold beef *anticucho*. Other ladies sold rice pudding in the evenings. Mototaxis and their drivers waited patiently in line for fares and read newspapers. Vendors sold candy and cigarettes. Every window and home entrance hid behind steel cages, most businesses, too.

Only a few blocks away, in the quieter neighborhoods, boys dressed as women sold themselves after dark. Broken glass and rocks covered the ground. Some houses were pieced together with adobe and sheet metal. Rebar stuck out of most buildings, and others seemed to melt into puddles of earth-toned rubble. Smog stained everything in a layer of soot. There were piles of stinky refuse on the sidewalks. Unintelligible graffiti decorated storefronts and homes. Somewhere in the bleak cityscape, my own death cried out to me from a street corner. The smell was exhilarating. I wanted to dance. I was there to play.

It wasn't all bad though. The construction was cheap compared to the U.S., but many buildings were well finished and painted often. There was a lot of movement and commerce there, so a fair amount of money. It was clear that the local government was spending money to improve the area. The grass in the parks was lush. Dominicos Avenue had a bike path all the way through it, with nice grass, benches, lights and trashcans. Some places were nice and well kept; a block or two away there was rubble and dirt and no grass. Developing nation was the perfect way to say it.

The sun never shines for nine months of the year, and it was Herman Melville who called it the saddest city in the world.

El Callao sits on a peninsula in the Pacific and is more of a slum to Lima than whatever mental images are evoked by its title: constitutional province. The Pacific coast of South America has no larger port.

Its history is hard and tragic, well reflected in the faces of the people who live there. El Callao and Lima served as the Spanish base of operations for the destruction of the ancient Incan civilization. Women and girls were raped. Men were enslaved. Everyone was indiscriminately subject to the cruel Spanish slaughter, and the trauma inflicted by the violence passed from generation to generation. To this day, the land is stained in the guilt of innocent blood proudly spilled by Conquistadors, and a curse sits on the city for the legacy of atrocities committed by its founders. They built cathedrals and colonial buildings as monuments to their conquest. There is no rain to wash it away, just dreary fog to keep the wounds moist.

Bloody rebellions raged in the 1800s. Throughout the 1980s and '90s guerilla factions terrorized the country in the name of communism. June of 1986 gave us the Peruvian Prison Massacres. No one was ever charged. Corruption runs rampant. By 1949 it had established itself as one of the biggest centers for cocaine trafficking in the world. That's why I got off the plane.

Back at Hostel Dax, I preferred the two English-speaking channels. The one-gram bindles came in grey wax paper, and I hid them under the TV between doing lines. It was a nice room for that part of town and had a private bathroom. Rooms could be rented for periods as short as 30 minutes. For three hours in my room, I peeked out of the window, watched the XXX movies playing on the hotel's closed-circuit channel and scribbled in my notebook.

When I finished the drugs, I walked a block and a half down Dominicos Avenue and found *El Vaquerito*, or The Cowboy in English. *AguaMarina* was a similar bar to its left on the corner, but it was closed. A *chifa*, or stir fry place, was still open to the right of *El Vaquerito*.

Cheap brown wooden tables with cheap brown wooden chairs were the only effects offered to patrons besides *cumbia*, cigarettes and liter bottles of Cristal or Pilsen beer. I sat at a table against the wall and lit my cigarette. The floor was filthy. Sad, dark figures sat slumped at a few other tables, drinking beer the way Peruvians do:

A shot is poured into one small glass. The bottle is passed to the next person in the circle. With a tap of the glass to the bottle, *Salud* is said and the shot of beer is knocked back. Whatever foam is left is poured into another identical glass sitting on the table. The process is repeated.

The song of a broken heart belted out in Spanish over lively trombones, synthesized drums and the tacky effects of a keyboard. *Cumbia* is always about unfaithful love and heartache, but it's great for dancing.

Too much cocaine furrowed my brow, and a cigarette stuck out unnaturally from my lips. The lady tending bar came from the back and saw me. I mimicked a bottle in my hand. She nodded and reached into the cooler for a bottle and carried two glasses over to my table.

"How much?"

"Tres soles," which is about $1.

"Here." Our eyes met briefly. Her dark features were kind. She lived in the back with three kids and her husband. One of the kids wasn't hers.

The shot of beer was cool and welcome. My head leaned back against the wall, and I blew cigarette smoke at the ceiling that glowed blue in the light of the bar. I snorted to clear my sinuses and thought about how much I hated myself. After a few more liters of beer, I felt like I could sleep and headed back to the room. In the morning I purposely overslept and missed any opportunity to fly back to Pucallpa.

Chino, the owner of the bar, told me his real name once, but I can't remember it. Sometimes, we called him Gordo, because his personality was as big as his belly. He had the nicest clothes and jewelry available in town. His white hat always looked brand new, and a braided gold chain hung from his neck. Everyone in the neighborhood knew and respected him.

He had been running those streets since he was 10 years old, while his mother sold bread and pastries on the corner out of a wooden cart. Over time they built their enterprise together, saved their money and rented out the two spaces on the corner of Dominicos Avenue, a block off Tomas Valle. His mother called hers Aquamarina after her favorite *cumbia* band. They made good money selling beer, and ceviche was available before 4.

When I finally woke up from missing my flight to Pucallpa, I went back to El Vaquerito. I ordered a beer with some of the money I had left, but in Peru almost no one ever drinks alone, so Chino came out to see me. He stood over my table and introduced himself.

"My wife said a gringo came in last night, but I was in the back, counting money." I drank my shot of beer and handed him the glass. He poured a shot.

"Well, I'm that gringo." I laughed. His smile revealed large gaps between his teeth. Any facial hair he had was thin and stringy.

"What are you doing here? You speak Spanish well." He knocked his shot back.

"Yes, I speak. I'm not sure what I'm doing now, but I've been in Peru for over a year, mostly in Pucallpa with the Shipibos."

"In the jungle, huh? You're crazy." Chino continued the conversation. He seemed impressed by what I was telling him but not necessarily in a good way. I poured a shot. "With witch doctors?" He shook his head.

"Crazy. Yeah. That is what they say, but I don't know. I like Peru. Do you know where to get any coke?" He said his brother would be by in an hour or so.

We continued to drink beer and got to know each other. He introduced me to his wife and kids. One girl was about 7 and her slightly younger brother was mentally handicapped. He liked to eat dirt and oranges without peeling them. There was a 2-year-old boy, who was very cute. Only the girl and toddler were his wife's kids, but she took care of all three. He had another baby, with a girl named Yolanda. She lived with his mother, because he didn't want anything to do with her.

After a while we moved to his mom's bar, where his brother was supposed to show up. He and I got drunk and smoked the cigarettes I bought. At mid-afternoon, four guys walked into the bar. They were younger than most other patrons and certainly louder. The guy with the ponytail was the most vocal.

"Hey, Colorado, what are you doing here?" Colorado means red in Spanish but is slang for white boy in el Callao. I preferred Colorado to being called gringo. In my mind it seemed less insulting. Mostly men called me Colorado. Women called me gringo.

"Nothing, drinking some beer." They menaced me with hostile tones and demeanor.

"I don't think you really belong here. This isn't the U.S. Maybe you should get going, Gringo." He had grease stains all over his jacket and pants.

"Maybe, I should." It was unnecessary conflict. "But, I'm enjoying this beer and these cigarettes and the *cumbia* playing. Maybe I'll leave. Maybe not."

He walked up to the counter and paid Chino's mother for the beer and another bottle. The men followed him out the door back across Dominicos Avenue to the all-night tire shop. They fixed flats and replaced tires all day and all night, seven days a week. Cocaine and beer helped them work the long hours. They were more of a neighborhood gang than guys who ran a garage, and I referred to them as *llanteros,* or tire guys in English.

"Hey, Chino, who was that guy?" I asked him.

"Pablo. He's a hoodlum. Thinks he's bad."

"Oh, do you think he likes me?" We laughed it off and got another cold bottle to drink. I paid for all the beer. Chino drank it. He was knocking a shot of beer back when his younger brother walked in.

Miguel was in a phase of laziness and getting into trouble. He had dropped out of school and didn't work. I heard all about it from the conversation Chino had with his mom.

Across Tomas Valle, Miguel introduced me to a mototaxi driver named William, who hid me in his mototaxi as we rode to la Huaca. It was by far the most dangerous part of town, and everyone told me not to go there by myself. The houses were small and some had plastic tarps instead of roofs. There were no sidewalks, only dirt and rubble everywhere.

The real name is La Huaca Garagay. It's supposed to be an archeological site. Besides a few rocks laid up by the hands of ancient man, some engravings and a deep hole in the rocks, there was nothing to see. Maybe it was a portal where evil leaked out of the netherworld into the neighborhood.

I only bought one gram and one more night at the hotel, because I was almost out of money. When I finished the gram that night, I returned to El Vaquerito to drink away whatever money I had left. Chino's six-year-old boy was throwing a fit on the ground by my table. So, I stood up and danced for him, but it didn't help.

Cumbia is a basic two-step, and I danced at every chance I got. The chemicals only helped. One Saturday night, Chino's wife told another girl I was the best dancer in the whole place.

Sarah was short, dark and pretty. We met at the *locutorio* she ran, where I made cheap phone calls, foreign and domestic. The clerk at Hostel Dax liked her, too. One night I saw her at the hostel, but she wasn't there to see me.

She and her manager at the locutorio let me make phone calls and pay them later. Someone had been stabbed to death right there, where she worked. No good reason for it, but the person died on the floor choking in a puddle of his own blood. Sarah's manager saw the whole thing. It had only been a few months.

There were a couple of computers, where I checked my email. A girl I met in another city sent me two or three a week.

They always started the same, "Dear Gringo, you are a savage. No one has ever done to me the things you did to me. When are you coming back, so I can see you?" She never got a response. I made long-distance phone calls to my family asking for money. The money always came.

"I don't know how long I'm going to make it, Mama,"

"What do you mean, Riley?"

"I think I'm going to die soon. Something bad is going to happen. I know it."

There was a pause on the line. Her voice was shaky but tried to reassure me. "Why would you think that? Nothing is going to happen, Riley. It's going to be fine. There is nothing to worry about." She must have known I was getting high with phone calls like that. It was before I started shooting up again.

"Someone is going to kill me. I'm sorry, Mama. I'm going to die. I love you." I hung up.

William's hook-up wanted to know who was buying so much *cloro,* as they called it. His connection found out and introduced himself to me. I was easy to find, because there were no gringos in El Callao. Mario only offered a slight break on the price but had a phone number and delivered.

"Do you know what my name is?" The night fog condensed on the windows of his station wagon.

"Mario, right?"

"You won't believe it, but my name is Mario Jesus." He stared at me. My eyes followed a lady walking down the sidewalk. His stared intently at my face. "Jesus. You know? Like Christ. Like the savior. I care about people." I rolled my eyes now.

"You know, Mario, don't take this the wrong way, but none of that sh*t is true. I don't believe in Jesus Christ. I don't believe he was God, and the Bible is a lie. So, I'm very sorry, but I don't care. I don't believe in that sh*t. Besides, Jesus didn't sell drugs. So what are you even talking about?"

"How many do you want then?"

"Seven is the magic number."

Paranoid delusions swallowed my mind in the hotel room every night. I squatted naked and sweaty in the corner of the shower. My hands clutched the heavy porcelain top of the toilet tank, ready to smash whoever came in through the windows. I would walk to Chino's bar to drink beer after that, sometimes hard liquor. Xanax and valium were available and extremely cheap. Chino and his wife trusted me, so I helped with cleaning tables, serving beer and selling cigarettes. I did it for free, while I came down.

But sometimes I stalked the streets at night jerking and twitching with evil in my blood, like a creature coming to eat children in the neighborhood. In America we have the boogieman, but in Peru it is *la pelacara*, or the face peeler. The legend was told to every child as soon as they could understand it, so when they saw me they ran. Mothers led their children to the other side of the street. People watched from a distance like they expected me to find a stray dog and rip his throat out with my teeth. I certainly looked the part. Hours would pass before I could talk myself down and return to my corner bars or the hotel to relax.

A short, fat woman in a black dress saw me sitting on a bench on Dominicos. She was about 50 years old. Money was gone till I could call home again. She asked me what I was doing and plainly told me she was a prostitute. I told her I didn't have any money for that kind of thing.

"You come with me for the night. I will get us a room and buy your drugs. All I have to do is go sell my phone to the guy who owns that place." She pointed a block away to the neon sign of a place that sold grilled chicken.

"I want some weed."

"Okay. How much do you need?"

"Like 10 *soles*." She reached into her bag and pulled out a bill marked with a 10.

In the room after I smoked a joint, she told me about her life. We lay on the bed with our faces inches apart.

"When I was a girl, as soon as I had breasts, my father would tie me up in the shed out back of our house, and he did whatever he wanted to me. And I mean whatever he wanted."

She looked up at me with tears and moved close. Most of her teeth were missing.

The condom broke and I spent 20 minutes in the shower scrubbing with soap, trying to wash away any disease. Afterwards, I left the room to go back to El Vaquerito for a while. When I returned at 4 a.m., she had checked out. It was the last I knew of her.

One night my tears fell three and a half stories to the concrete below. For some reason, I was on the roof of Hostel Dax, where they hung the bed sheets to dry. My toes hung off the ledge, but it didn't seem high enough. I decided not to jump.

A cabbie picked me up on Tomas Valle and took me to another part of town for some powder. Two guys walked back into a hole in the side of a building to get it. It looked like an earthquake had cracked the building in half. After that I cried. The taxi driver didn't know how to handle it and dropped me off as soon he could.

Two guys ran the late-night stir fry joint next to El Vaquerito. The owner called himself Disaster, and he had a lot of women who came to see him while he watched his business. They would sit at the table and dote over him.

Negro was from Ica, on the coast, and said he missed it. He cooked. The food was salty, greasy and cheap, an ideal snack after a night of drinking, and the sign said Chifa. A curly-haired girl with dark freckles all over joked with patrons and waited tables. She teased me to give her a baby with green eyes.

"Hey, Colorado, are you hungry?" It was one of the colder nights, and the fog rolled in. I hadn't eaten or slept in days. Disaster showed me kindness with his offer.

"Yes. I can pay you back."

"Don't worry about it. Negro, make him some rice."

"Oh, Gringo, you want some rice, huh? Well, let me get you some." Negro smiled with big white teeth. He made me laugh every time we talked.

Soon after that a crowd spilled out onto the sidewalk in front of their restaurant. I couldn't see what was going on at first, but Chino's mom skirted the crowd with me and looked worried. Two men held Disaster's arms behind his back while Pablo swung at his face. Disaster's braces tore his cheeks, and blood hung in black ropes from his chin.

I pushed past the crowd with ease and flew into the conflict. In my mind I was a 400-pound silverback. Before I knew it Pablo and I were IN the back of the restaurant, tearing a table apart as we fought on either side of it for a grip. The two other men offered no threat. Everyone watched. Chino's mom barged in and broke it up. She grabbed us by our collars like she was holding two kittens by the scruff. The men promised me death, and the scene dispersed. The freckled waitress told me I was strong and asked me if I was crazy.

"Let me see it," Chino said. I covered the dislocated pinky finger of my left hand with my right. It was obviously dislocated. At the second knuckle, it bent backwards at 90 degrees. He held my hand and leaned down to examine it.

"This is really bad. Wow." He laughed, and in a split second he pulled it with all his might. I screamed.

"What are you doing?" My voice broke. He laughed at me in the backroom of his bar.

"How else was I supposed to do it? You weren't going to let me if I told you."

"True. Well, thanks." I chuckled for relief from the stress. It was still mangled, only slightly less. "Those idiots need to be stopped. They can't be doing stuff like that. Why wasn't anyone doing anything about it? Disaster is a nice guy, and the whole neighborhood just sat there watching it. I think Pablo does like me." I smirked. A stupid smile on his face, Chino didn't say anything.

"Maybe because they don't want to get killed later, when they are least expecting it." The silhouette of Chino's mom in the doorway declared with matriarchal authority.

"She knows what she's talking about. Listen to her," Chino said. His mom left as soon as she saw I was okay.

"You are good people, Gringo." Chino's wife walked over to him and put her hand on his shoulder. One of the kids was at her feet. In her soft Spanish, she said, "You're a good guy, but you need to forget about it. You don't need to be messing with that. Now go home and go to sleep. You've had enough for the night. We'll see you in the morning."

"Hueco! Quiero hueco!" Chino yelled at his wife and grabbed her butt as I walked away. I turned back to look. Her calm face never changed expression, as her drunk husband made his vulgar demands. Hueco means hole.

I found a pharmacy that sold vials of liquid valium for cheap, so I bought a needle for it. I quit snorting cocaine. With the needle, my mind disintegrated. The cops were always about to bust me. It was common for me to be on my knees in the middle of the room with my hands behind my head and screaming,

"Come in! I surrender! I have no weapons. My hands are on my head! I won't resist!" I didn't want them to think I had a gun so I put myself in the most vulnerable position for them, but they never came.

The family that owned the pharmacy where I bought the vials were horrified to see me back the next day attempting to buy several more. It was too much for one person to do, but I persisted and settled for two before I left.

My mind was not sound. I was hygienically challenged anyway, but cocaine and pharmaceuticals exacerbated my condition. One morning I found a huge smear of what proved to be human excrement on my sleeve. Hopefully my own.

"Do you have a boyfriend?"

"No." Her tone was a mix of disdain and disinterest.

"Do you want one?"

"No. Even if I did, I wouldn't want you, loco." Leticia had a lighter brown complexion, almost red, and big, thick thighs she stuffed into the top half of her jeans. Her legs were crossed, so I reached over and pinched the mound of flesh above her knee. Her body shifted forward and her face radiated. She restrained herself from slapping me.

"Don't ever touch me again. EVER! My legs are mine. Keep your hands to yourself."

"Sorry. You have nice legs. I didn't mean anything by it." She relaxed and our conversation continued.

Leticia was single at 30. She was a virgin, which was unheard of in El Callao where infidelity was the way of life. Her family was good and Christian. We got to know each other because she worked in a different locutorio on the other side of Dominicos. I had never been to it before, but I owed money at the locutorio where Sarah worked. Since Leticia had seen me around, she trusted me to pay her back, and after that I only went to her locutorio. I walked her home one night and met her mother, who was sick.

It never made sense to me why Leticia talked to me. Green eyes, like mine, are a novelty in a country where 99% of people are brown-eyed and brown-skinned with black hair. Maybe it was a bad boy thing. I was kind to her but bound by addiction and violence in the streets. Such contradiction in a man draws women.

"Sueltame" by Grupo Nectar was a cumbia song we both liked and sang together sometimes when we talked at midafternoon in her store. Our knees touched when we sat. "Let me go. Break the chains. I don't want to live like this" are the lyrics. It was about a break-up, but it described my chemical bondage well. I brought her cookies when I came to see her.

The name of my favorite cumbia song was *"Ojala que te mueras,"* or "I hope to God you die" in English. It played loud in El Vaquerito, while Miguel told a story about how he and his brother Chino had defeated a group of four men. We were talking about my violent exploits. The incident with Pablo had incited in me a hunger for brutality. I had developed a habit of talking trash to groups of young men who were no strangers to violence and hated gringos. After several close calls, I had ended the previous night hanging from a car window going 50 miles an hour, because the taxi driver didn't want to give me a ride, and I tried to jump in through the window. Eighteen-year-old Miguel boasted how tough his family was. Chino waited to speak.

"That was a long time ago." Chino looked at me. "Fighting is how people get hurt. Around here, that's how people get killed. One blade or one bullet on an unlucky night is all it takes. Then, you're dead. You need to stop, Colorado. Everyone can die. Those guys across the street. Me. Him. You. Everyone." His thick finger dug into my chest and his face twisted in emotion.

"No one messes with us, huh, Chino?" His little brother insisted.

"Shut the f*ck up. You don't know what you're talking about."

"Chino is mad, because his woman is giving him problems. Then, he's got Yolanda and her kid hanging around the family businesses like a couple of sick dogs." It was a cruel thing to say about the mother of Chino's illegitimate child and the kid. She hardly had enough sense to take care of herself, much less the baby.

Chino jerked up and reached over to slap his brother. His meaty forearm and open palm swung short because Miguel was falling backward out of his chair. Miguel ran to his mother's bar.

I went to visit Leticia one evening. Her desktop computer was in pieces. The door to one of the phone booths was on the floor. It was Pablo's routine. First Disaster, now Leticia. He never hit her but scared her for money. I puffed up and punched the wall. She asked me to stop in a quiet voice and walked close. We squeezed each other in a long embrace.

"It's okay, Riley. It will be okay." She was the only person who knew my name and pronounced it well.

There were only two things I ate for those few months besides cookies. *Anticucho* is a marinated beef kebab, usually sold with tripe and grilled right in front of you on the street corner. It is delicious and sold at night by women making an extra dollar for their household. Most of the women who sold it laughed when I came to eat. It was not uncommon for me to eat 10 skewers in a row or more.

The other dish I ate was ceviche. Ceviche is originally Peruvian, not Mexican, and it doesn't involve tomatoes. Cubes of white fileted fish are cooked by the acid of lime juice. Red onions, a hot pepper, light seasoning and salt, toasted corn kernels, steamed sweet potato and a piece of lettuce complete the dish. These elements all mixed together was what I loved. The first time I ate it, I couldn't believe how good it was. Peruvians don't eat ceviche after 4 in the afternoon. It has to do with the freshness of the fish caught that morning. Inca Kola is a yellow-colored cream soda, which I drank with my ceviche.

Other nights I wandered the streets looking for danger. I knew the territory north of Tomas Valle well. There was La Huaca where dirt and rubble covered the ground and getting robbed was a guarantee, and I knew 33rd street where the boys dressed like girls sold themselves. They injected silicone or baby oil directly into their face and butt cheeks to soften their jaw lines and square hips. Some of the prettiest girls you will ever see are not girls.

Back in another direction there was an apartment complex where the courtyards turned into a zombie apocalypse every night from 12 to 4 a.m. Never have I seen anything like it. They smoked pasta basuca and drank cheap wine. Someone pulled a woman's hair. Incoherent verbal altercations teetered on the edge of physical violence. A glass bottle smashed on the ground. Everyone twitched and jerked around for the pasta, clucking like malfunctioning mechanical chickens.

I walked to La Huaca at 4 one morning to score. It was stupid, and the house all the cocaine came from didn't want to sell me anything. On the way back three men tried to strong-arm me, but I presented more scrap than they cared to deal with. An old lady watched through the bars of her bedroom window. She said something, and they ran away.

The first light of day was in the sky and several mototaxi drivers had pulled over to watch the commotion. Only the hood of my jacket was torn off. I raised my hands in victory towards the spectators on the side of the road and screamed in Spanish something like, "Did you all see that?"

Mario heard about it and came to see me the next evening after I had slept most of the day. I bragged. He complained about the hard time his hook-up was giving him for my going out there. He yawned while I bragged about how tough I was.

"Look at my eye." He pulled off his glasses in the car parked on Dominicos in front of a restaurant called La Braserita. It was right next to the hotel where the prostitute had gotten us a room that night. The red and orange lights of the electric sign came in through the window and lit up the right side of his face.

"Do you see it?" Milky blue scar tissue covered half of his brown iris. "I used to fight in the streets. I got hit with a big stick. They say they can remove it, but I don't have enough money for the surgery. Fighting comes with a price."

There was a 10-foot drop from the second story balcony of Hostal Dax. I just jumped. No stairs. The owners hated it and didn't understand, but they knew I was crazy. A combination of my years on skateboards and the chemicals running through my blood made me agile and stupid. I pushed the limits of it like everything else and lived out delusions of being some kind of superhero protecting the innocent. I climbed the sides of buildings and shimmied up street lamps with ease. I was a crack-headed spider man. More than once, I perched on a street lamp in broad daylight, high out of my mind, and pretended that my life was a comic book.

"What's wrong with you? Where is your shoe?" Mario asked through his car window.

"Nothing. I'll tell you right now. Everything is fine." We were meeting for the daily quarter ounce. Sometimes we met twice in a day.

"What do you mean? It doesn't look like everything is fine."

My hands and feet had bled all over from too much cocaine. Every line and crease in my palms and on the backs of my knuckles was dried out and cracked. It was like a curse out of a Stephen King novel. Blood dripped down my hands and soaked into my socks. No one I saw had an explanation or words of comfort. Chino stared sideways at what he saw. What words comfort someone willfully killing himself with chemicals? It was eerie and scary. My right foot throbbed and stung, so I took my shoe off before I met up with Mario.

"Why is your shoe off?" I showed Mario my hands and foot. "You don't need any more coke today. I'm not giving you anymore. Go home and go to sleep." I didn't have money at the moment, and he was fronting me the drugs so it was hard to argue. But I planted myself in his front seat until he gave me some. I got one gram before I left.

In the dark, the light of the TV flickered blue on the walls and over my skeletal frame. Blood flowed into my syringe before I pushed off, alone in the corner, and the curtains fell with me 8 feet through the open window to the flight of stairs leading into the lobby. I landed on my back and slid to the bottom. The ringing in my head got louder and louder. Shirtless and barefoot, I made the nine-year-old boy check the room for intruders. There were a few streaks of crimson down my arm mixing with my sweat, and the boy's parents kicked me out.

I spent the rest of the night hiding behind cars parked on the side of Dominicos and jumping out into traffic. Headlights swerved and tires screeched. Spanish curse words flew out of the open windows, while drivers leaned on their horns. Finally, I passed out in the grass of the median. It was the most comfortable sleep I had in a long time.

The life of the neighborhood continued as it always did on those nights. Pedestrians walked the bike path and around corners. Disaster's chifa was open for business. The freckled waitress laughed with patrons. One of Papillon's songs played loud through the door of El Vaquerito. On the corner an older lady and her husband sold anticucho the same as every night. They were Christians. Some of the younger people drank outside of the bar. Two or three together, they shared bottles of beer.

One of the llanteros was talking to two girls. We had exchanged words earlier that afternoon, so I walked out to the bike path on the median of Dominicos and offered him a chance to get crazy. I called him a coward and insulted his mother. It was obvious he heard me, but he was scared. His body language said it all.

A few hours later, they got me on the corner of Tomas Valle and Dominicos. It was Pablo who led the attack. El Callao was a suicide mission, and it was over.

I dreamed it would be my bloody masterpiece of pain and destruction, because these were my gifts from the world and all I had to give back to it. It was a piece of art in my mind, the messier the better. Pain was my life and death was the end of it.

But it was no fun getting turned into a chunky puddle of my own brains and blood like that on the sidewalk. There was only one person who knew my name in the neighborhood. I could only think of my mother. Rocks ripped into my scalp. A rope of white snot hung from my lip. Light flashed across my field of vision. Shame was all I felt. It was impossible to scream, but inside of myself, I screamed with all I had.

There had been something like 20 brawls in the two months since I first fought Pablo in Disaster's restaurant. Fights weren't about bragging rights or boxing. They were about seriously hurting another person, even killing him. This one was about murder, my murder. A shot was fired.

El Callao, Peru
Summer 2008

"Poppa, what was it like when I was missing in Peru?"

"We thought you were dead. Must have been about 10 days of me and your mother looking at each other and not saying anything. Finally, we broke down and cried."

Remember when I said getting bludgeoned to death is not as much fun as it sounds? Of course, it isn't fun, and that's a ridiculous statement, but playing with the prospect of a brutal and untimely death had been an exciting game for me those 3 months in El Callao. When I realized it was not a place where people played, it wasn't fun anymore. Looking back, my narrative is full of ridiculous statements, like that whole "pain and destruction were my gifts from the world, and all I had to give back to it" bit at the end of the last chapter. That was what I felt and thought, but I can't figure out how I came to such an absurd conclusion.

"Get off him, you idiots." The hold on my legs and arms loosened. There were no more cracks on the back of my skull. A cop had shot his gun and screamed at us. "You almost killed that white boy. Get off him! Idiots! Gringo, run home."

In the U.S., an ambulance would have picked me up, but in El Callao, I was lucky to walk away. It was a miracle that the officer was there in the first place. The iron-rich stink of blood filled my nostrils, and the feces that had run down my leg became a cold, uncomfortable mess I could do nothing but ignore. I limped into the Third World night. My brown hoodie hung torn down the back, so I threw it in a trash can. There were two vials of liquid valium in my cargo pocket, and in the bathroom of Disaster's restaurant, I checked them. One was broken. The other was intact.

Back in the hotel room, the chemical warmth of liquid valium helped me relax enough to try sleeping. It smelled and tasted like a hospital, astringent and sterile, but it was not enough to do much with my tolerance as it was. I passed out from exhaustion.

When I woke up the next morning I walked up Dominicos to see Chino and his family. I stayed sober for a few days and ate ceviche and anticucho every chance I got. I hung out on Dominicos and Tomas Valle.

I had beers with Pablo. The beating created a bond between us, because he was crazy like me. I didn't have a clique to back me up, but he respected my lack of fear. One of his friends told me I was lucky I didn't get killed. In El Callao, they pack iron. He meant guns.

Mario found me on the side of Chino's bar one afternoon and asked me if I was lucid. He was in the neighborhood and drove by, probably because I had not called in a day or two. It was the warmest day of my time there. Chino's daughter jumped rope on the sidewalk, next to me. I still have a pencil drawing she did for me of me and her standing under a rainbow. Almost a decade has passed.

"Your eyes. I can see in your eyes, you are lucid. Sober. That's good. That stuff is bad for you, Colorado."

"Yes. I'm well, Mario. It's nice to be sober."

"I'm happy to hear that. Call me, soon."

I had called my mother and told her that I had almost been beaten to death with rocks. She didn't seem surprised. She sent me enough money to last for a few days since I was not buying any coke, but a few days later, the rent was due. So my grandmother sent me some money, because I told her I was going to get a job selling cleaning chemicals to hotels and restaurants and needed shoes and clothes, besides living expenses. In an hour, I picked up a Western Union for 300 dollars and got a room at the Dax.

It took me an hour to score in the park a few blocks away, as dusk settled over the commerce and traffic of the Callao district. Mario had given me my usual order of seven one-gram wax paper bindles. Back in the room I unwrapped one and poured it into the plastic spoon.

Before the black rubber plunger hit zero sirens were singing high-voltage harmonies of evil in both of my ears. It was the grievous poison of the thing I chased hardest and hated most. I sat on the step into the bathroom and smeared the droplets of dark blood down my arm. Perspiration formed on my temples and along my uncombed hairline. The caustic fumes of chemicals floated out the back of my throat. A stampede of antelope ran through my head, and my eyes shook. My jaw tried to unhinge itself but settled to cock itself sideways and hung crooked off my face.

I stood up. Greasy cargo pants hung raggedy off my skinny waist. A dingy shoestring pulled two of my belt loops together. I swayed, panic stricken in the middle of the room with odd posture, one shoulder slightly stooped. There were six more grams on the bathroom floor. I picked them up and swallowed them, wax paper and all.

The shot of cocaine opened an invisible portal in my room that night, and the screeching whistle in my ears turned into weeping and wailing moans of tortured souls. Dark voices breathed out murderous threats against me from the other side of the abyss. Or maybe the voices were coming from the other side of the chain-locked door. I couldn't tell anymore.

I jerked to the wall where the light switch was. The voices morphed into intelligible banter between cops over hand radios about me and what I was doing as they planned their raid. My hands fumbled at the switch. The lights went out.

In the dark, demons crawled through the portal and into my head, through my nose, eyes and ears. There was an urge to puke. My heart beat too hard, like it was going to explode, like always. The shadows of feet stepped back and forth in the crack of light under the door. Pablo was in the room with me, and he had come to finish the job. His hand touched my arm.

I turned the lights on. My mattress, bed frame, the dresser and night stand barricaded the door. It was supposed to help me relax while I was high, but now I pulled the furniture off the wall and walked out of the hotel onto Dominicos.

I found Leticia, at work.

"I can't close the store yet Riley. It's too early, but if it is slow, like it is now, I can close early. I'll take you to a sober house. Don't worry." Her face focused on me. She had fallen in love and wanted me to get help, but the shine of cocaine evil in my eyes put her off. We had never talked while I was that high.

After a couple of Christian guys talked to me for a half-hour or so, she closed the locutorio. Four of us walked a good distance down Dominicos to a place I had never been. The men knocked on the door, and some men from inside let us in. Wood grain panels covered the interior of the office. It was nice, much nicer than the back where the clients stayed.

"Gringo, let us show you the place. Come back with me." Two of the men led me back. Leticia stayed there with the guy who ran the place at night. I gave her the rest of my money and went to see what they had back there. We hugged goodbye.

"I'll see you tomorrow, Riley."

In the back, everything was made of white-washed cinder block and rebar. The cement floor looked cold and most of the men were already in bed. They showed me a bed, second from the bottom; the bunks were four high. I didn't believe that people climbed to the top, but warm bodies snored and drooled on their pillows up there. Sleep came easy. I never thought about it.

Breakfast consisted of two pieces of rock-hard bread with half a cup of weak, warm tea. The tea made the bread edible, because it was too hard to eat otherwise. There was no free space with all the men and the tables out, so we kept them folded up and against the walls during the day. They only came out at meals.

After breakfast, we stood in crowded lines to pray and sound off. Pseudo military kind of stuff. The 12 steps were in Spanish on the wall, but this place was all about Jesus. I hated

Jesus. I heard the facility director say, "This is from Monday to Monday. We don't get days off from fighting our disease." We stood for an hour or so, then we had some free time to shower and smoke and talk.

The bathroom had two pipes that came out of the wall and poured cold water into two plastic barrels. Water only came on for an hour in the morning and an hour at night, so we stored it for bathing and flushing the toilets, which were nothing more than the bowl with no seat, no tank. There was always an inch of cold water on the floor, and hints of raw sewerage pervaded the air.

Many of the men entertained themselves with playful teasing and trading food their families had brought them. Others sat solemn in the corners on benches, smoking quietly. Others still were intrigued by my presence. An old man with wet brain, named Lucho, antagonized the younger men with a plank from his bunk, and they called him names. I leaned against my bed and met the guy in the bunk beneath me. His name was Gamarra, a black guy, and he reached his open hand out to me.

"So, you're the new guy, huh? And how did you get here? Gringos don't run around here." He looked me up and down and pinched my shoulder, as if to point out that I was a skeleton. "Well, I know how you got here, like the rest of us. None of us were much more than a dirty dish rag, when we showed up. I'll take care of you while you're here."

Much like the jails throughout Latin America, this faith-based rehab barely fed you. It was up to your family to bring you food, and Gamarra's family brought him a lot of food. He took good care of me out of genuine love and compassion. After I had been there for a few days, he sat me in a chair and shaved my face except for the mustache. He said it made me look like a businessman, and we laughed. I traded him my dirty Columbia jacket for a shirt, and we talked often.

As that first day continued, I noticed that when the other men had their shirts off, they showed thick spider webs of white scar tissue all over their backs and shoulders and arms. I had heard once that when people smoked pasta in a circle a knife was passed right behind the cigarette, so the men could slash themselves. The desire to stab or slash one's self was something I understood well.

Lunch was scant, maybe a half a cup of quinoa and some tea. Afterwards, they packed us into the dormitory so some of the men could have visits. The facility was overcrowded to begin with, but when they stuffed 45 of us into a small dorm room, it got worse. My legs and back turned into rubber bands, and beads of sweat pushed through the pores on my face. I tried to watch some Jamaican gangster flick, dubbed over in Spanish, but I kept remembering that my parents needed to know where I was. They had heard from me four or five times a week for months now, sometimes every day, and the last thing I told my mother was that I had almost been murdered. She would worry soon. Several days had already passed since we talked, so I packed my backpack, put my jacket on and started to walk out through the main room, where men kissed their wives and visited their kids. Before I got to the curtain and out into the visiting room, 10 guys rushed me and pushed me to the back wall. Soon a sea of men stood before me, my back against the wall.

    I tried to explain the situation and that my mother needed to know where I was and that I would be right back. They didn't buy it, but then I explained that I had checked myself in and would check myself out. The director, a 28-year-old guy named Pingo, stood in front of the crowd talking to me. He had a life of violence in the streets of El Callao written on his face and eyebrows with scar tissue even in the way he held his shoulders.

    "What do you think you're doing?"

"I'm leaving!"

"No, you're not! Who is checking you out?"

"I checked myself in last night, and I'm checking myself out now!"

"NO! You're not going anywhere!"

He shoved my shoulder back against the wall lightly, and I shoved back. The sea of men rushed me. They pulled my arms and legs apart and covered my nose and mouth so I couldn't breathe, but I never passed out. Then my hands were hogtied to my feet behind my back with my own blue shoelaces, and I screamed. They threw me on Lucho's urine-stained mattress. I struggled to catch my breath on my stomach, with my hands and feet in the air behind me. They threw *La Santa Biblia*, or the Holy Bible, in front of my face. They all believed deeply in Jesus Christ's deity and in the sanctity of La Santa Biblia. Disrespecting it or denying it was not something they ever saw people do. Even the most violent and murderous criminals in the ghetto knew that it was the Almighty's word. I cleared the phlegm from my throat and spat directly onto it, before I called them all a bunch of, "b*tch mother f*ckers" in English.

One of the men fanned my face with a notebook, and once I calmed down they untied me. I was quiet. There was nothing to do but go with it. I couldn't win. I was defeated in a way I had never felt before, deep within, a surrender to the hopeless and miserable captivity in this Third World, Christian prison made of whitewashed cinderblock and rebar.

Not once in my three-month tirade could I remember coughing, except when I smoked weed, but now I found myself with a deep, gut-wrenching cough that kept me and everyone else awake all night; after a few days of it, they let me sleep in past six a.m. I felt like there was a madman driving a maul into my chest and stomach, all day and all night. It never stopped, and eating the stale bread was only possible between fits. My ribs and abdomen were too tender to touch, and it occurred to me that I didn't know much about tuberculosis.

I had read about it and knew they called it the consumption back in the day in Ireland and Europe. It was a bacterial infection that affected the respiratory system, but I heard of it getting into people's bones. These were the conditions and the kind of place where people got it. I knew that much, and I wondered if this would be the end of me.

I got out of bed after a few days and dragged the tattered backs of my pant legs across the floor with a lethargic shuffle. Some of the other men made fun of how slow I was, but there wasn't much I could do about it. The cough and lack of calories, besides the other abuse I put my body through with the drugs and violence, were catching up to me. All I could do was pretend like I still had fight in me when they laughed. There was nothing inside but exhausted defeat and desperation.

My first night moving around, I couldn't breathe for some reason, and I grabbed the top of a partition with my hands and hung, trying to expand my chest. It was terrifying; my lungs refused to pull in a breath. Tears rolled down my cheeks, and the men watched me, helpless. It lasted ten minutes as I gasped for air. We all assumed it was asthma, related to the cough, but I had abruptly stopped consuming unheard-of quantities of oral benzodiazepines, not to mention four or five intravenous injections of liquid Valium that I had almost every day for two months. My tolerance had been such that I didn't feel anything when I did them. The guys who ran the rehab bought me an inhaler, but night after night my lungs wouldn't expand and my throat closed.

When a new guy came in, I would catch him picking crusty scabs out of hair on the back of his head. I knew what he was doing, because I picked the scabs off my scalp as well, from where Pablo and his gang had beaten me in the head. My pinky was still mangled, swollen like a balloon in the middle and refused to straighten out. Different men would talk to me about how I got there or what I was going to do. They were not quick to share their cigarettes with me because of my coughing. I tried to tell them that I had to leave, but no one listened. Unlike in the prisons in Peru, rape was not allowed there, but I could see it in the eyes of some of the men, crossed with perversion and violent lust, twisted like the eyes of fictitious cartoon guard dogs. Two brothers had been there for seven years.

"They let me out twice," one guy told me, "and both times I went and smoked pasta as soon as I got out. They had to carry me back here."

"When is the last time they let you out?"

"About three years ago, at Christmas."

"Well, three years later, what will you do if you get out?"

"Smoke pasta. It's better if I stay here."

After almost two weeks of being there, I realized my only chance of getting out was to start a fight. It was one of only a few facilities in the country where they didn't beat you or use violence as form of punishment. Starting a fight got you kicked out, not beat up, so I started one. There was a kid who was fat and short and when we listened to CDs of worship music, he got on the ground and faked tears and remorse. I grabbed him by the collar and pushed him against the bed when he laughed at me one night. It was all I could do to pretend I had it in me to hurt him. I was tired.

Several other men saw it and came in to break it up. Pingo told us to go meditate, which was punishment requiring us to put our noses to the wall and hands behind our backs. The short kid was crying, and I apologized to him.

"Sorry, man. It was nothing personal. I needed to be heard." I laughed.

"What do you mean?" He turned to the other men around us and whined, "he said he didn't want to fight me. He did it for no reason."

The other men and Pingo pulled me off the wall and asked me what was wrong.

"My mother and father think I am dead! Leticia is not my wife! She can't be in charge of my committal! I need to leave, and this is the only way I could get anyone to listen!" I pretended I was tough still. "Besides, if I wanted to fight him he wouldn't have any teeth right now."

They asked me if I wanted to leave in the morning or that night, and I chose to stay till the morning. I stayed up late and watched the new Batman movie, a bootleg dubbed over in Spanish. As soon as I woke up, ate breakfast and stood in assembly they let me go, and I walked the two blocks down Dominicos, across Tomas Valle to Leticia's locutorio. It was right next to where the llanteros worked. She was happy to see me and let me make a phone call.

I dialed the country code, 001, local area code, 504, and the remaining seven digits of my father's veterinary clinic. He would be at work, and I was excited to talk to him. I knew he would be worried, but I didn't realize how much. The line rang, and the digital meter added ten centimos for the call so far. It rang again, and his secretary picked up,

"River Road Veterinary Hospital. This is Beth. How can I help you?"

"Beth. It's Riley. Is my dad there?" She had known me since I was a little boy.

"Yes, he is. One second, Riley." The phone was silent as I waited for his voice to come in over the line.

"Riley?"

"It's me."

His voice twisted and choked before he asked me,

"Do you know what it's like trying to figure out how to tell your wife that your only son is dead?"

They had been paying a man named who knew me and worked with Timothy on the movie to identify my body in the morgues of Lima. It wasn't a question of whether I was dead, but whether they would find a body. My father told me to go to the airport to meet up with the man who had been looking for me and he would take care of me until I got back home.

Leticia took off from work and came with me to the airport, and we met German, the man who had been looking for my body. He took us to eat ceviche and got me a hotel room, until we could figure out how to get my stolen passport replaced.

Leticia came and stayed with me in my room for an afternoon. We watched an American movie, and she told me she liked tango dancing, like the characters were doing on the TV. Soon, I exhibited one my most heinous and natural traits.

I put her in an emotional arm bar, until she gave me what I wanted. I pulled her boots and pants off and kissed her for a moment. It was long enough to realize that her teeth were mostly metal in back, and I pictured kissing a Terminator as the metal scraped across my tongue. We kissed a moment more, before I jerked my head away from her, denying her the tenderness she wanted. As my interests moved lower, her hands and body language cowered from me. My thoughts were filled with the coarse texture of the skin on her dark thighs. I liked her legs better in jeans before she gave herself to me and I made scathing judgments of her body. It was quick and I was not gentle. She screamed in genuine, physical pain, as I denied her my lips and any emotional reassurance. When I was done, I picked myself off her and put my pants on. She tried to make eye contact, but I refused. She rolled onto her back, still naked and shook, visibly distraught and ill. The sheets were the only cover she had between her gaping heart robbed of its innocence and the derelict who pillaged it.

No communication but the squeaks of a speechless hurt from the back of her throat attempting to maintain the appearance of dignity. Her brown eyes swelled with desperation and longing to connect with mine the way they had before this tragedy, before she lost it all. Now, I blew cigarette smoke at the ceiling, lying in bed next to her with my shirt off, and watched TV. She had to climb out of bed to get dressed in front of me on the floor, and her arms and head hung in shame as she pulled her pants back on. I ignored her until she left. Hurting people is what I did, the deeper the cut the better, and I didn't have to try to do it. It was my genius.

German took me back to Pucallpa to wait for a month, until the embassy would have my expedited passport ready for me. Marina and Teo saw me once before I left. I didn't touch cocaine before I left but smoked weed and took benzos. My parents had not allowed me to come back home for the last year and a half, but now after I disappeared and someone WAS looking for my dead body in the morgues they were ready to have me back.

I never saw Chino, after that, but I wondered what happened to him and if he ever thought about me, that crazy gringo who saw him almost every day for a few months before he disappeared forever. I have asked myself if he talked about me. His mother's health was bad before I left, almost ten years ago. The picture his daughter drew me is in the same black leather binder, with all the rest of my dark, cocaine-fueled ramblings and drawings etched in black pen. Leticia asked me to get some medication for her mother, which was cheap in the U.S. My dad had access to lots of it, something simple, but I never delivered. Her mother was in great pain without it.

Over the years, I wondered if it all really happened, or if it was some dark indie suspense thriller about drugs, violence and a death wish. Sometimes, it seems like a dream I had a long time ago, distant and difficult to remember, a beckoning and visceral dissonance. Anytime the cold damp of a heavy fog falls where I live, I see Chino's smiling face and can almost hear the thump of cumbia playing. It was a time when black magic conjured a violent evil in my life, and I opened portals to hell in my head and hotel rooms every night with vicious hits of cocaine. I almost pulled it off, almost shocked the neighborhood with the sight of my mangled, murdered body. I mocked death and even breathed in its cold permanence before I played hard to get and made my escape. We weren't finished with each other. There was more to our story, and we would play this game again.

New Orleans
2008- 2009

I had a room in an apartment on Octavia and Fountainbleau. I kept it pitch black all day and night. My bare mattress sat against the wall. A heavy comforter hung from the curtain rods, and in the corner a reading lamp sat on top of an unplugged TV. It was the only light in the room, and it focused on the only things that mattered to me: a spoon, a syringe, a lighter and some empty baggies. Cigarettes and hot spoons had melted the black plastic top while I dug around in my forearm searching for a vein. Sometimes I sprayed the bloody water on the walls.

My room matched my head, rotting trash strewn everywhere, curtains stained with bodily fluids, stink and neglect. It was full of a black sickness and wherever I went, I painted everything the same color. Things could be going well, but it would not be long till I turned my life into a mushroom cloud and everything around me into rubble. Once again, those who loved me would be left to shield their eyes from the shockwave of brains and shrapnel that would otherwise hit them in the face.

I loved to make a mess.

I struggled to order my food in English at the airport in Houston, partly because I had been living in Peru for so long and partly because of the Xanax I took before the flight. My family stayed positive about my arrival in light of the fact that I barely escaped El Callao with my life and in spite of the fact that things looked to be much as they always were. Timothy came with my father to pick me up from the airport to get some shots for the movie which they were still doing although spottily. I slurred my words.

My mother invited Turkey and the rest of the family and friends to see me at the house after my 18 months in a foreign country and longer than that exiled from home by addiction and being categorically uncivilized. My dad bragged about me to his friend in the pool one night.

"Hey, Derrick! Riley was a street fighter in the ghetto down in Peru." That was an exaggeration, but I had been in a lot of fights.

He always looked for the positive side of things, which was remarkable because he had had someone looking for my dead body in the morgues of Lima a month before. As far as he and his friend were concerned I was the kind of person they only read about in books. He admired the way I rejected societal pretenses and anything I couldn't justify as having substance, but his heart broke when he saw me living like a slave to chemicals.

"You don't give into anything! I look at you and see a resolve I wish I had. It's like where does that even come from? Then you turn around and give your life to pay for your drug dealer's Cadillac. It doesn't make any sense, Riley. Can't you see it?"

I was smoking crack and shooting heroin within two weeks of being back home and couldn't eat Thanksgiving turkey from doing meth. There were times when my mom would send me to the store to buy three packs of cigarettes with a 20-dollar bill, but I wouldn't come back for an hour and a half, without cigarettes, without money and without a reason why. One night my dad caught me crawling across his bedroom floor to get his wallet out of his jeans, and I put a hole in the kitchen drywall when he screamed at me. A week or so after that, he got mad at me while I was still in bed, so when I got up I shattered a 3x6 glass table top and smashed one of his cherished reel-to-reel players. Carlos met me in the park that morning, and after a half-hour my mom showed up to say that she was done being taken hostage in her own home. I told her that I hoped she died and called her a b*tch and flung an extinguished cigarette butt at her face.

My mom paid a friend from grammar school $450 to rent the back half of his apartment on Octavia and Fountainbleau. She wanted to get me out of the house if nothing else, and my roommate was on an indefinite suspension from his career as a local police officer after flashing his badge and beating up a pizza cook when he was drunk one night. My roommate always bought two bags for $100 but I got three for $120. He snorted his and looked down on me for shooting mine. On several occasions, something they used to cut the dope gave me an allergic reaction and caused my hand and arm to swell like a balloon with hives. I asked my dad if he had any ideas about what might cause my arm to swell like that, but it only made him look worried.

I figure this is good a time as any to tell you about my parents, where they're from, how they met and what life was like for us in the city of New Orleans. Not only will this give you some important insight into the lives of two major players in this horror show, it will be a nice break from these gross displays of selfish brutality toward people who loved me. I imagine reading this can be hard for someone who's never been there. It's hard for me to write, sometimes.

My mother was Miss Catholic High growing up in Baton Rouge. She went to St. Joseph's Academy, which is the sister school to Catholic High, where my father went. They didn't know each other, and it would be years before they finally met in New Orleans at his cousin's apartment. My mother had a hard life growing up. Her father drank. Her mother spanked. She learned to take care of herself early on and carried that into our family. There is no one who ever taught me to believe in myself the way she did.

My father was a Chapman by name, an American by birth and a veterinarian by trade, and he became a father at my birth. We have a mixed heritage a bit Irish, Scottish and English, marked by fiery tempers. No one can get angry like a Chapman. Many have said so.

My father went to visit his dying first cousin a few years ago, one of two sisters who were deformed from birth. He told my sisters and me about them a few times in my life. My uncle and grandmother mentioned them a time or two, in passing. I never saw them and never thought about it much, probably in part because my father never really seemed too concerned with it. His life continued with us and my mom and work and the bills and making memories to last him the rest of his life. He was successful. In spite of struggles, he came out okay, but the night he went to visit his cousin on her deathbed and his aunt with all her mental faculties sharp as ever, he broke down. I wasn't there, but my mom told me he had to run out of the room, because he was so openly and uncontrollably sobbing. He and I never have talked about it. I never asked why, but I have my doubts that he could even give a real answer to the question. That's my guess, because I'm subject to similar episodes.

Maybe he wondered why her and not him. They were about the same age, but here he was coming to visit. He came to get a half-hour glimpse into the life of his cousin who'd never experienced the things she should have. She was about to die. She had no kids, no husband, never made love. That was her life, and it was ending in that room. It's not fair. It's just the way things go, and it can be enough to make a grown man cry.

As I grew up, he spent the night drinking with my mother, dancing in the clubs or with friends at the house. We had babysitters a lot. They loved to party and entertain the local musicians, but sometimes drinking turned into arguing. Arguing turned into things I wish never happened. I cannot adequately describe how much I love my parents. No one is responsible for my actions except me. But I will say this: while alcohol is a loved thing for so many, it never caused anything but problems in my household growing up.

Life on heroin continued for me in New Orleans. My father made a deal with me on a Monday morning behind the clinic. He would give me $50 a day to stay well until I could get enrolled in a methadone program. I should have checked into it that day, but I got high and slept. On Tuesday morning, I didn't go see him about the 50 bucks. Instead I broke into my parents' house and stole a big box TV and some jewelry, which the pawn shop wouldn't take. I would have to try for another 50 bucks from him.

"You said you were going to find out what you needed to do to enroll in the program if I gave you that money! Now you want more?" His bottom teeth stuck out of his mouth, and there was a V-shaped crease in his forehead. Nothing expressed disappointment the way his green eyes could.

"I know. I'm really sick." I sat in the Land Cruiser and clutched my stomach with the window rolled halfway down.

"I don't think I can help you today. Sorry!"

"Well, then, go get me a bottle of the pink sh*t!" I slammed my elbow through the driver side window and cut the wheel all the way to the right. I ripped my foot off the clutch and slammed onto the gas to spin backward. He rolled behind a parked car to protect himself. The pink stuff was his euthanasia solution for putting animals down.

I spun circles backward in the gravel parking lot for a while and jerked the vehicle to a halt and screamed at him through the broken glass saying that I would drive into the Mississippi River and kill myself that way. He was on the phone calling 911 as he followed me down to the river behind the levee by the clinic and back over it again. When the cops showed up I cooperated. They used soft restraints, because my hands and arms were bloody and swollen from thrashing around in the vehicle. The 911 call can be found on YouTube with a search for "A Crooked Line," under the user TungstenMonkey. First, you'll hear my father talking to the operator, and then you'll see footage of me getting arrested on the side of his clinic. I don't remember it but according to Timothy I had called him out to the clinic to meet me and when he showed up the cops and ambulance were detaining me, so he filmed it.

My mom and dad found the stuff I had stolen in the back of the Land Cruiser but did not press charges. The hospital sewed me up and required me to spend the night on the psyche ward of Ochsner Hospital. There was nothing they could do for me. They let me go in the morning.

Somewhere I found a maroon turtleneck and wore it everywhere I went. My beard had grown bushy and red. My hair curled and sat thick on top of my head. My belly pushed the fabric of the turtleneck into grease and cigarette ashes and made it protrude so that cola and cereal fell on it when I ate on my bed at night. I looked like Zac Galifianakis in that stained turtleneck.

Timothy came over to film, so there was some footage of me at the apartment talking about how I didn't get high anymore, "just well," but I am nodding out in the shot and scratching my nose wearing the turtleneck. I tried to fold my clothes on the bed but instead I leaned over them half asleep and rolled them up into wrinkly balls, before putting them into my suitcase. It was the most absurd thing you've ever seen. I said,

"Well I'm a piece of sh*t, so I hope nobody is too disappointed about that. I'm a sorry piece of sh*t."

I worked as a valet at one of the hotels on St. Charles and went to work that next Saturday night as usual. If I made enough money in tips while I was working, I would take off with one of the customers' cars to score in the ghetto, but that night was not good for me. My mom's mom, Grand Mary, let me stay at her apartment 10 blocks away, because I didn't have the Land Cruiser to drive back to my place.

In the morning I woke up with my legs on the wall, and when she came to take the sheets off the couch, she asked me if I wet the bed.

"No."

"Then why is the sheet so wet?"

"I'm sweating."

"Why are you sweating?" She reached out to touch the moisture on my forehead.

"I'm sick."

"Why are you sick?"

"Um... I'm sick for heroin."

"You're on heroin?"

"Yeah. I'm on heroin. I'm sick."

"Why did you get on heroin again?"

"I don't really have a good answer for that, but I get sick, so I can't really stop."

"Well, what are you going to do about that? Isn't there something you can do?"

"Yes. I'm supposed to be getting on methadone Tuesday morning."

"Why wait till Tuesday?"

"That's when they take people into the program."

"Hmm. Well, how are you going to work?"

"I don't know. I can't get anything without money."

"How much money do you need?"

"Bags go for 50."

My grandmother went to get her wallet and took me in her Camry to the Conoco on Willow before she took me to work. I was so high at work that I almost got fired.

More and more the place on Octavia fell apart, even though I had started the methadone program. Dried out chunks of a once stringy slime and mold grew on the dishes piled high in the sink. There were two vases of dead brown flowers on the kitchen counter. Half of a plastic grocery bag had melted to the stove top coils. I lost my key one day and smashed through the front door window. Broken glass sat scattered on the floor until I moved out, and the toilet had clogged weeks before I left. I kept using it anyway, and waste mounded out and above the rim. The TV sat on a table in the hallway and blocked anyone from getting into my room without some serious maneuvering. I used a broom to change the channels from bed, and since there was nothing for me in town and no one who wanted me around I talked Carlos into letting me move back to Taos with him in a few months. I'm not sure if he ever actually agreed to it, but that was the plan.

After being on methadone for a couple of months I wanted to wean down for the move back to Taos, because I didn't know where the closest clinic would be or how I would get there. There was a counselor assigned to my treatment program at the clinic, and he looked terrified to see me at his door asking for counseling. His button down shirt didn't fit right. He had a bowl-cut haircut and a chipped tooth. It was clear that he had no business being an adult, but here he was responsible for helping me get off some seriously addictive chemicals.

"Do you think we could lower my dose, maybe 10 milligrams a week, so I can get off the methadone?" He looked like a first-grader without his homework and squirmed in his seat. He stared at his lap and shuffled the papers on his desk around. "Um, why don't you let me make a call?"

He used three fingers to push multiple buttons at a time and struggled to hold his half of the alleged conversation. I wondered if he was a real man or three Little Rascals on each other's shoulders pretending to be a grown-up. He seemed lumpy enough. I expected the beeping that lets you know the phone is off the hook would be coming over the line any minute. I walked out.

My parents helped me get some suboxone from a dealer. I took my last dose of methadone on a Monday morning and let half of the orange stop sign-shaped suboxone dissolve under my tongue the next morning. A wave of queasiness rolled up from the soles of my feet. Another wave rolled down from my goose-bumped scalp and the two met in my abdomen. My stomach quivered. I became a soggy burrito under my covers. Calf muscles burned like I had the flu. Sleep came in five-minute increments of fevered terror. There was an invisible piece of hair in my throat, and I let another piece of suboxone dissolve under my tongue. Nothing changed. For three days I experienced precipitated withdrawal, which is when a full agonist, such as heroin, is displaced from opioid receptors by an antagonist, such as naloxone (Narcan). In other words, if you don't wait long enough to take suboxone after your last dose of any other opiate, you experience full-blown withdrawal, immediately and for several days. There was nothing I could do about it.

While I waited to go back to Taos I had to move back into my parents' house for a month after the landlords evicted us from Octavia and Fountainbleau. One morning, I noticed my dad's hair was gray. He looked tired. The passing years and his only son had aged him. I had not slept in a day or two, but I could clearly see the price of my selfishness that day. Quiet, he walked through the kitchen. The lines in his face and straight lips said it all. He cast his eyes down, and he stooped. I was killing him.

The sight of it hit somewhere inside of me I didn't know existed. I got a momentary glimpse of the pain he lived with, and it was more than I could take. For a few hours every time I looked at him I busted up into tears and had to run outside in fits of uncontrollable sobbing. He was wounded by my self-destruction. I had always wanted to hurt him for whatever it was I held against him, but now I didn't know how to turn it off.

It would not stop, because inflicting pain was second nature and came without thinking. We were stuck with it, and I cried my eyes out.

He didn't say much, and I don't know if he understood what was happening. Sometimes drug addicts cry for no reason, and I had not been sleeping. My moods were unstable especially around him, or at least he always noticed the instability. I weep now, when I remember what he looked like that day. Stuck with a reality he hated. He chose to suffer quietly while his guts twisted, and his son chased an early death.

My last week or so in New Orleans before Carlos took me back to Taos I continued to maintain my opioid addiction with crumbs of suboxone and talked to people who weren't there from the meth I was shooting. On the last day there, Carlos and I were loading up his truck to head to Taos where I would start again. I told my dad my new idea for a book.

"You know, Poppa? There is a lot of beauty in being buried under the shale in a nameless grave on the side of the mountain, so the pigs can eat you." I was sincere and enthused. We both liked to read a guy named B. Traven, a Marxist writer down in Mexico from the earlier part of the 20th century. He had written of his desire to be buried like that for the pigs, a truly socialist sentiment. "I'm going to call it, 'Bury Me in Taos.'"

"Why would you say something like that, Riley?"

My dad didn't think my idea for a book was so beautiful, but he was happy to see me go with Carlos. To his dismay, Carlos and I came back to the house a few hours later. I locked myself up in my sister's room and dug around in my arm with a horse needle until blood covered me. My dad knocked and almost busted down the door before I let him in. Downstairs in the kitchen my mom fried catfish for my uncle and aunt and Carlos; I freaked out on my dad.

"This is why you can't be around, Riley. No matter what you are always upset about something. The way I look at you and everything else!"

Carlos and I took off shortly after and made it to Lake Charles before we stopped to sleep at a Motel 6. I wish I could say my behavior reassured Carlos about my coming with him, but I kept talking to translucent figures in the dark of the room and looking through the window. When we woke up it was miserably hot and bright, and the anxiety over the carnage I left New Orleans sat in my stomach like hot chunks of lead, until we got to Taos.

Taos

2010-2011

A guy named Zeke had his place on Kit Carson in the shade, where I met Turtle Tom and most of the people I knew in Taos, like Garth the Dope Whisperer and Jolene, Timmy, even Thad and Luanne. We sat on raggedy couches in the living room cooking up shots of heroin or cocaine and pretended we were all friends by candlelight. A 16-year-old blonde and her Sid Vicious boyfriend smoked crack and lived in the attic while Zeke stumbled around and gawked at the bushes behind his house with blood running down his arm and his jaw unhinged. His 6-year-old daughter sat on her bed in the dark until the authorities came and took her away.

That was the second time I lived in Taos.

Carlos and my mom helped me get my truck back after the incident in Santa Fe a couple years before that when the crack dealer took it and never returned it. They also helped me get a place on the side of the highway north of town toward Arroyo Seco. It was an old office building we rented from Carlos's friend, who apparently had money and property but terrible hygiene and the propensity to make awkward and perverted statements at the worst times. He stank but he was a nice guy and let me rent the place for $600 a month.

Someone shared the news about Doh-Doh's death with me. The old red head named Becky was nowhere to be found. The hoodlums at the park and plaza all had different faces and names. DVDs of "Where the Buffalo Roam" and "Young Guns" entertained me on a cruddy laptop someone gave me, until I got a job washing dishes at a restaurant called Ogelvie's. I called my father bored and depressed with nothing to say and choked back cries for help he couldn't give me. He thought I was sober. My parents sounded very happy about how well I was doing.

I bought a copy of "Hell's Angels" by Hunter S. Thompson, and like so many drug addicts, I idolized him. My father had given me a typewriter like Thompson's before I left New Orleans. It was my most prized physical possession. Thompson had inspired me by getting published as a journalist who placed himself amid the dangerous Hell's Angels for his book. In similarly dangerous fashion, I wanted to document a group of Mexicans crossing the border illegally but decided the potential of being baked to death in the back of an 18-wheeler was not worth getting published. Besides, I couldn't finish reading "Hell's Angels" once drugs came around, much less organize and document an illegal trip across the border from Mexico. The mental stability and concentration necessary for that kind of thing simply did not exist in my life.

They say the books you read, movies you watch and people you hang with form who you become. It was true. A fascination with Billy the Kid, Gonzo journalism and doing drugs while living in the New Mexican desert had heavy influence on how my life would play out over the next few months. Besides, Taos is a crazy place.

There was a 16-year-old runaway from Florida who held a cardboard sign at the light on the north side of town. He hooked me up with meth. We called him Tweaker Bird. I met my boss, Thad, who also had connections for meth and cocaine. We laid flagstone during the day, and at night, I washed dishes at Ogelvie's. A guy named Timmy and his dog came to live with me around then. I had a few other friends who smoked weed and usually met them at the Plaza Caffe, which was supposed to be a place for hippies, but we chased paying customers away with our body odor and grease-caked pores and blew hits of weed at their kids. We badmouthed the owners for selling out and never bought more than a cup of black coffee with refills. One day, my new friend Travis came to find me at the Plaza Caffe.

He needed a ride for his uncle. I had no problem giving his uncle a ride, but Travis didn't have an uncle, at least not in Taos. We all knew that.

"Sure, I have to be back to work at Ogelvies for four."

"Cool. He's back at Zeke's. We have to get something out of his car."

Minutes later my blue S10 idled in the shade of Zeke's gravel driveway. It was my beautiful blue truck once again (until I forgot to put antifreeze in the radiator. Then it was an immovable eyesore that the grass grew around in the front yard of Carlos's house on Montoya. The death of that truck marked the death of my alleged eight-month stint of sobriety. It was more like four months, and I smoked crack and meth the whole time.)

"Tom's 73 years old and from Woodstock. He showed up earlier this week and flipped his car down a ravine two nights ago. The highway patrol said he flipped it at least six times and walked back up himself. A real miracle. He had to throw his stash and scale before he could walk back up." I pretended not to notice that Tom was not Travis' uncle at 73 years old. "We just have to help him get something out of his car, in Questa."

Before my hand came off the horn, an old man busted through the screen door with a bob and swing in his walk, an exaggerated limp. The racket of the door creaking open and clacking shut mixed into his belligerent squawking. There was no one except us, but he made accusations. He muttered curse words under his breath like he was spitting in disgust and climbed into the passenger seat. Travis squeezed between us.

"F*cking imbeciles! I've never seen anything like it in my life. Just a pile of horse sh*t!" Over time, I would learn that this was his default. Ninety-five percent of the time, he was this way, unless you had some coke or heroin.

"I know. I know," Travis replied. "I talked to Zeke about it. He said he didn't know anything about it and blamed it on Christine. I don't believe it, though."

Some drama I wasn't privy to, but I found out later that Tom's dog was missing. It was one of two times Zeke and his girlfriend, Justine, had stolen and traded the old man's pure-bred Pekinese for a bag of cocaine to Freddy, a diabetic drug dealer in a dirty double-wide on the south side of town. He was unusually sweaty. His face looked like he was sucking a lemon, and the only hair he had was a werewolf patch on his right shoulder. Deep-pitted boils of brown covered his skin from his bald head to the stained waistband of his shorts. His shirt was always off. His health was always terrible, and he was always sweating.

(Once after Freddy moved to the north side of town, I saw him getting wheeled into the emergency room. I spent a lot of time at the hospital back then, and since I knew he was going to be checked in for a while, my friend and I burglarized his house. It was blatant and my S10 ran out of gas a quarter mile down the highway. Besides the safe, with some silver dollars and a couple OF ounces of high-grade weed in it, the only thing I got was rinses out of his dirty heroin cookers. That was the main reason I broke in. We walked up to the Conoco and put gas with the silver dollars into a milk jug. His neighbors saw us do it, but Taos is a land of outlaws, and cops are rarely called.

Eventually the old man's dog got eaten by coyotes in the sage brush behind my house after he moved in with me. The old man had bad luck.)

"Tom, this is Riley. Riley, this is Tom."

"The indomitable Turtle, they can't keep me down! Turtle Tom Stone! Pleased to meet you!" His tone and attitude completely changed. It was a show he put on; after all he was an entertainer in Woodstock, where he lived before and used to do drugs with the bass player of The Band. He stood in for Levon Helm when he was sick, because they were both singers/drummers. Levon couldn't stand Turtle, though. He thought Tom was a piece of garbage.

We passed a pipe full of green hash and coughed, crammed in the tiny cab. Tom coughed hardest. He was 73 after all, but when he coughed a weird sound came out of his chest, like a marble rattling in a can of soup, probably from the wreck in the ravine. Travis looked at me horrified. Tom acted like he didn't hear it and took every hit he could. On his move to Taos, he had stayed in a hotel in Iowa where the toilet broke in half while he sat on it. The water damage was so severe that they wanted him to go to jail. Somehow, he lost his U-haul trailer with everything he owned because of it.

As we finally got out of town, whatever heroin Travis and Tom did before they found me mixed with the hash to soften the lines in their faces. Their mouths hung open and their chins were on their chests. The silence of sublime sleep filled the cab, but for the hum of fifth gear. To the left a vast expanse of desert territory summoned my imagination. They said Taos was still the wild, wild West, so I listened for the busting caps of antique six shooters and the thud of arrows through the necks of cowboys, shot from the bare backs of painted horses. Somewhere in the distant dust was the war cry of dark men with long hair and a caravan of covered wagons burning. It was faint, but I could hear it before the road dropped into Hondo and back up toward Colorado.

Funny how people are when they ask you for something, especially junkies. Tom wasn't Travis' uncle. He made it sound like his car was down the street or worst-case scenario in Ranchos, but not 20 miles away in a different town. There was almost no way I'd be back by 4. Travis nor Tom had any clue where his car was, not a number to call, not the name of a junkyard, nothing. It may not have even been in Questa, and I bet anything that whatever they wanted out of the car wasn't in it anyway. But that's how it goes for a junkie in Taos.

At a gas station we pondered what to do. Tom didn't have any ideas. Travis was busy smoking heroin in the bathroom, and there are untold junkyards in Questa. Tom and I sat in the truck and smoked cigarettes waiting for Travis.

"Why don't you go in and see what's taking him?" It had been over 20 minutes, and when I walked into the gas station Travis was on an office chair behind the counter. His face was green and body doubled over. He held his gut with his hands.

Before I got back out the door an ambulance pulled up. They loaded him onto the gurney and into the back. It was a bad case of gas as far as I could tell, from his diet of pure sugar and the irregular bowel movements of an opiate addict. A gloved hand grabbed a tube of lubricant and a rubber tube in the window of the ambulance before they pulled away. I shook my head and walked back to the S10.

"Well? What the hell is taking so long?"

"Ambulance came and took him. He looked like his gut was in a knot."

"Ambulance? Really?" The truck was 15 feet away while they loaded Travis into the back, but somehow Tom had missed it. "Are you sure? I guess he won't be coming back with us then."

"No. No, he won't. Probably what he ate gave him a stomach ache."

"What did he have?"

"A giant moon pie and a bunch of orange soda."

"Well, no sh*t! What did he think was going to happen? Eating like that! F*cking imbecile!"

Tom got silent and turned away as if he forgot what he said. He looked out of the passenger window, pensive and still, pondering some deep truth about life. Dark clouds gathered over the horizon, and the aura of heroin and his tiny pupils were peaceful. His long grey hair barely touched the collar of his leather coat. It was proof of the wisdom only 73 years of life can give.

The crinkle of cellophane broke the silence in the truck. He pushed it back before his dentures ripped a chunk of moon pie into his mouth. The gold handle of his cane rested on a 64-ounce fountain drink between his legs.

"F*cking imbeciles, I tell ya! I've never seen anything like it in all my life. Well, let's get going."

I started writing about Tom as soon as he moved in. My plans were for a book. The first line went,

"The heartache. The headache. The stink of watery, green feces sprayed on the walls and puddled on my landlord's carpet." The carpet was new when I moved in. Brand new, and Tom ruined it. On top of my plans for a book about Tom, I had dreams of being a poet at that time of my life. It took me years to realize I hated poetry.

Tom began to detox in a bad way. It was the beginning of a dramatic and obscenity-laden affair of about two months. He kept a welcome mat on the floor next to his bed, and I picked it up out of curiosity one day. Underneath were at least nine black rectangles where cigarettes had burned from end to end on the carpet, but the mat was also completely caked with green poop. Between the toilet and his bed, the green trail proved he was not well. There was a spray of lime green on the wall by the door.

Tom was a self-proclaimed junkie through and through. He knew it. He told so many stories of all the dope he had done and where he did it and how good it was and who he did it with. Those days were gone though, and 73 is not so kind to a junkie.

We were all dying like him. It was only more obvious that he was on his way out. Dead men and dead women walking, we looked for life in death, because staring death in the face was the only time we felt alive. Everywhere we went, our environments changed to match the death inside of us, but we lied about it to ourselves and to everyone else. None of us believed it, but we lied about and pretended this was what we wanted.

We did meth and heroin and smoked cigarettes in his room, dubbed the shooting gallery. Tom needed a medical detox, but he had a habit of saying he was going in and not doing it. I dropped him off before a six-hour shift at Ogelvie's one morning. When I came back to the house, I went into his room to find information on how to visit him at the facility, but he was sitting in his bed smoking a cigarette.

"How'd you get out of detox? Or did you ever go?"

"They kicked me out."

"They kicked you out? Why?"

"Too much trouble. They said they weren't prepared for me. Too much sh*tting. Too much runny nose. Said they didn't expect me to be sh*tting all over the place like that."

On another morning I opened my eyes to see him sliding his thermal underwear over his foot. It was the first thing I saw, and the fabric got caught on his big toe nail.

"Come on, you f*cking b*tch!" He screamed at his underwear and pulled harder. He ripped the big toe nail out of his foot.

Tom had become my main focus in life. He and I laughed till we cried at night in his room. We told each other stories about our lives growing up, but besides him, I had relationships with other people. The majority of my friends claimed to be spiritual in one way or another. Everyone in Taos does, but since I knew these people, I assumed it was a symptom of their mental illness, which caused them to think joblessness, drug use, refuting science and bad hygiene placed them on higher moral ground than the rest of the world.

There were a few different girls who came around, one named Luanne. Some people tell you they are bipolar, and others you find vacuuming your living room at 4 a.m., dancing to dubstep and smoking a bowl of weed, even though you know that they don't do meth. Luanne was that kind of bipolar, and she spent the night with me sometimes.

I saw another girl who panhandled change in the parking lots during the days and had my mother's name. She was beautiful in a weathered kind of way like some old mama you find at the pound, worn and scarred by the world but beautiful because of it. Tom affectionately referred to any of the women I ever brought around as "that f*cking whore."

My friend Timmy and his dog were the sanest of anyone living at my house. He only smoked a little heroin and meth and frowned when I locked myself in my room for days watching pornography on Luanne's computer. I smoked cigarettes at the living room table, sweating in my underwear, and jabbered at him about my plans to start a mobile pet crematorium or the mystery of repeated nucleotide sequences in DNA with no discernable purpose. Timmy nodded in agreement to anything I said. He knew better than to disagree with me.

Anytime we went somewhere Tom told strangers of the abuse he suffered at my house. It was humiliating and largely untrue, but one hipster kid bought Tom's line and sneered at my inhumanity. He would take Tom to his house in Tres Piedras and care for the old man as any decent human would. The guy made a big show of how altruistic he was and what a disgrace I was. When I saw Travis later and told him about the kid taking Tom to his house, we laughed so hard that we had to put our hands on our knees to keep from falling on our faces.

The next morning, I found the two in the hipster's Nissan in the parking lot behind the Plaza Caffe. Tom sat in the passenger seat with an unlit Native 100 between his lips and acted excited to see me, too excited, like he needed something, like things weren't working out with the hipster.

"Hey, Riley! I'm so happy to see you!"

"Hmm... Are you now, Tom?"

"Oh yeah! Extremely." He turned to the hipster in the driver's seat. "Hey, you! Where in the f*ck is my phone?"

"I don't know where in the f*ck your phone is! It's your phone! Why don't you keep track of it?" I agreed with the kid. It wasn't his responsibility, and they yelled some more before the old man came back to my place.

Tom got healthier while he lived with me, and my heroin habit grew. He put on weight and got his bodily functions under control for the most part. After two months it was time for him to leave, and he had a place rented in El Prado. I packed his stuff into the back of my truck, and for some reason he called me a, "f*cking piece of sh*t! You know that? A real piece of sh*t!"

After all I did for him, I had it. I had only ever touched him with care and concern. All the times he went to the hospital, I visited him. When he came back from a CT scan, I patted his head and held his hand. At night before he slept, I washed and rubbed those two petrified pieces of mahogany he called feet and lathered them with tiger balm, but now I had him by the collar, my fist cocked back behind my head, and bit my lip. "Oh what? You're gonna hit a sick old man, are you? Bet you feel real tough! Don't you, boy? You're real tough, now!" I threw his boots into the back of my truck and took him to his new place. My back tires sprayed him with muddy snow and gravel as I tore back out of his driveway.

My manager at Ogelvie's asked me about him a week after he moved out.

"He said he thought he was bothering you a little bit or something."

"A little bit?" We both laughed.

Tom came in on a Saturday afternoon to watch his Iowa football team play Ohio. Tiffany, my manager, said he kept walking around the place "grabbing himself." She called me to come watch him, and in case things got crazy I could take him away.

Ogelvie's fired me for acting goofy when I came out of the bathroom at work. I wore sunglasses to wash dishes and had a weird film that collected in the corners of my mouth while I obnoxiously ranted at customers. A week after that I defaulted on rent at my place. When my landlord came to see me, we talked for 30 minutes in the cold next to a shattered front window while addicts lurked around inside. He was nice about telling me I had to go, but when he left, I found a loaded syringe behind my ear. The weather had already cracked the engine block in my S10.

This is when my parents found out I wasn't sober anymore and I had to move out. I called them for money. There was no real reason to tell them about the dope, except I thought I might try getting sober and figured telling them didn't matter if I did. My mom talked to me. She told my dad later.

The summer after fifth grade I started cleaning horse stalls for my dad. He paid me $5 for four hours of work every day and $20 the next summer. By the time I was 13, I had $1,000 bucks in my sock drawer and spent it all in a few months on weed. My father and mother did so much for me in life. They taught me such good things. Here I was again to tell them I had thrown everything away.

Before I moved out, Tom called me to tell me he had broken his hip and that he was staying in the old folks' home by the hospital. We hadn't talked since the day I almost punched him, so I went to visit him.

"Yah! Fell on the ice on the road up to my house coming back from the movie store."

"What did you rent?"

"I don't know! Some flick about a hit man. Whatever it was, it wasn't worth shattering my hip. That was it, though, when I fell. I couldn't do anything, and it was getting dark. The neighbors drove around me and up to the house to watch TV! Can you believe that? Drove right around me lying on the ground! I could have died!"

I smiled. It seemed hard to believe, but unbelievably bad things always happened to him. Now he graced the nursing staff of the geriatric ward with his red faced, foul- mouthed, screaming accusations. They caught him rolling around in his wheelchair smoking weed in the hallways. He liked to pretend the pictures on the wall were fine art. When he didn't get what he wanted from the staff, he messed himself and rolled up to the nurse's station and demanded they take care of it.

"Well, I'm glad you're not dead, Tom. I missed you."

"Missed you, too, Riley. Missed you too. How's that piece of sh*t? What's his name? Timmy? Can't stand that mother f*cker. When is he going to get where he can take care of himself? I mean. He's only 38." Timmy and Tom never liked each other. Neither of them seemed to like anyone else for that matter.

"I don't know where he's going to go. I don't know where I'll go for that matter."

"What do you mean? Are you getting thrown out?"

"Yeah. I decided to buy some coke last month while the rent money was in my pocket. You know how it goes."

"Yeah. Yeah, I do. Ha ha. F*cked yourself, didn't you?" He showed his dentures with a smile.

"Yup."

"Well, I won't be home for a while. At least another month. You can stay there and help me out when I get back home."

"Awesome! Thank you!"

"Just one thing, Riley."

"Yeah? What's that?"

"Leave Timmy wherever the f*ck you found him in the first place. The last thing I need or want is his sorry a** at my place. Lousy piece of sh*t." Before I left, I told Tom I loved him. It was something I told people back then, but to me love only meant that I wouldn't rip you off unless I had a good reason and the cigarette I bummed you last month entitled me to half of everything you owned for the rest of my life.

There were a few days of wandering in the cold and staying at Thad's house. I moved into Tom's place a few days after Thad stabbed me in the face with an umbrella over a handful of Xanax I stole from my friend's leukemic landlord. Despite all that I had going against me in terms of reputation and appearance in town, the black scabs on my face embarrassed me, because they made me look less than sophisticated. Looking sophisticated was the least of my worries, and while Tom was in the hospital, my new friend Johnny and I tied my mattress to the hood of his car to move me and Tim and Tim's dog into Tom's new place.

Tom ran Tim and his dog off as soon as he got home from the hospital and fell in a pile of his own feces soon after that. In an episode of dementia, he had gotten mad at me about not giving some syringes to Johnny and yelled for help all night long after he fell. I let him sit in it until the morning, even though I couldn't sleep for his yelling. It was a heinous thing to do. Heinous was what I had become. He struggled to breathe for several days before we took him to the hospital, and it turned out one of four broken ribs had punctured his lung. His lung had been collapsing. He snuck his IV out of the hospital when they released him, but when he pulled it out at the house, his blood was black sawdust.

Sometimes I banged out reams of nonsense on my electric typewriter like a maniac firing a machine gun. Sometimes I decided that the world was ending and that I would die soon. There was no point in writing, then. Sometimes I stayed in bed and watched the squares of white sunlight slide slowly across the floor and up the wall until I couldn't take it anymore and had to get up to figure something out. Sometimes I yelled at my dog from all the stress Tom caused me.

I forgot I had a dog, until now, but I probably wouldn't have told you about him anyway. My career as a dog owner was a disgrace, and I thought if you hated me any more than you already do, you might stop reading. Not that my neglect of the old man two paragraphs before this one shouldn't make you hate me enough to stop reading, but these days people seem to value animal life more than human. Let me tell you about my dog. He was a good dog.

It was Thad who brought him to my place after finding him in the KTAO parking lot some months earlier, and he was mostly heeler, what we called a Taos Cattle Dog. We named him Serio, in part because he seemed serious and in part because Sirius is the dog star. It fit well, and he understood me perfectly. He would leave at eight in the morning and return at night. He could sit, stay, lie down, get on the bed, get off the bed and anything else I asked him to do. He never went to the bathroom in the house except this time I screamed at him in my bedroom, and he pooped on my bed. It was clearly intentional and made me laugh because I deserved it.

When I moved from my old place to Tom's, I overdosed on anxiety meds and left Serio outside of Smith's grocery store. It took me several days to realize that he was missing, and when I did, an empty leash tied to the railing at Smith's was the only thing I found. Serio showed up at Turtle Tom's the next morning, even though he had never been there. It was an amazing feat and endeared me to him more than ever.

Now, I can't remember if these last few paragraphs are about my dog or the electric typewriter my dad gave me. Either way, they were both destined for doom like everything else I cared about. My typewriter slid slowly off my bed even though I could have stopped it. I was too depressed to move. The impact shifted the keys, and it never worked again. Another local drug addict took Serio from me. Of course, he was better than I was and accused me of neglecting the dog but shot him for killing one of his chickens a week later. Such was my life and all I touched.

"Everything the warning labels on prescriptions say not to do is everything you want to do!" Tom laughed with his dentures out, like he was channeling my old friend Doh-Doh. With tears in his eyes, he told me of entertaining back when he was Turtle Tom Stone and made crowds swoon. He told me that every time he died from an overdose and went to heaven some "Abe Lincoln looking mother f*cker" sent him back saying he had to come in the front. That he couldn't come in the back door.

Turtle said he once woke up in a refrigerated room under a sheet of plastic. His clothes sat in a bag on his feet and he had a toe tag. He got dressed and found dope hidden in his waistband. The whole hospital was frantically searching for his missing body, while he snorted drugs in a bathroom stall. His friends already had all his stuff and were squatting in his apartment when he walked up. A soothsayer in Woodstock told him this was his last incarnation and that he was paying the price for the evil of his past lives. These were the stories he told me.

One day he watched our friend's girlfriend open his window and hang her belly over the sill before she slid onto the floor. The lights were off and she supposed he was gone, but Tom watched the whole thing from his bed a few feet away. She came for the flat screen. Tom slapped her in the head with his cane and used his walker to escort her to the front door. That was Taos when I knew it. Your friends robbed you and talked bad about you when it didn't work out for them. Tom sent me to the bank to pull 40 bucks out of the ATM and get some cocaine one night, but I took $300 out of his account and never came back. The year's last snow had still not melted.

I slept at the homeless shelter after that. My friends all lived there, too, and walked the parking lots with me during the day asking for change. When we injected cocaine in the vacant lot behind Albertson's, they all hated me for abandoning them, gnawing my cigarette or licking kerosene from my lips as I walked away. A cop stopped me panhandling once and took me to jail on a warrant for an old ticket I never paid when Serio got loose. I spent 12 days in jail. It should have been one night. The afternoon I got out, I used a lint ball out of my sock to filter a shot of heroin and got cotton fever. An ambulance picked me up at the homeless shelter. I puked and screamed. My head throbbed. The ER tried to kick me out at 4 a.m., but I cried in the waiting room until they let me back in to sleep.

When the weather got warmer, I slept in a burned-out trailer or the bushes behind an auto parts store. My sleeping bag stank of chemicals and rotten eggs. I left my bag and clothes in the bushes during the day. It was my camp, but one day someone defecated on all of my stuff. Whether it was malicious or not, I didn't have time to wonder, because I had to find a new place to sleep.

When the weather got hot, I would end up at that desert oasis in Ranchos called Taco Bell. Inside I stared at the walls painted red and purple to make it look less cheap and listened to the soft jazz. The dropouts working the counter understood the plight of life in Taos and let me drink the cold Baja Blast with a water cup. I pondered life and what could have been and what was not. Tourists stopped in to eat as they passed through town. Their kids complained that their sister did this or that and wanted to know the next time they would swim in the over-chlorinated pool at the hotel. I would close my eyes and imagine that I was one of them on a road trip with my family in late July. Back-to-school commercials on the hotel TVs offered deals on binders and loose-leaf and pencils. Anxiety put knots in my stomach when the commercials played, and I could feel it all, like I was there and nothing had ever changed, like I was 11 years old again waiting to start the sixth grade. Then I would push the door open and walk the highway miles back to the Albertson's parking lot looking for a fix.

Johnny and I used to tear through Taos in his white Lincoln Town Car with two other kids while I projectile vomited out of the passenger window. Both of those kids are dead now. One jumped from a cliff escaping imaginary and malevolent figures. The other overdosed and got left in his car at the ER one night. They found him dead in the morning.

Other times Johnny and I hung out with an older nurse who hated me until we shot cocaine together. Then she stripped down and danced and sang for me while Johnny and I laughed at her. She never noticed that I wasn't into it, but that didn't matter. She was into herself. It was common to watch her mix way too much cocaine with way too much heroin in the same shot, and 10 minutes later she bragged about how she only ate granola because Fruity Pebbles were so unhealthy. She told us about a house she had in Ranchos that was haunted by a patch of red paint that bled through multiple new coats over several years. Eventually she had a dream set in the same bedroom in which details were disclosed about a 19th-century abortion involving a teenage girl and a priest. I tried to contact her about the story, but she's dead too.

My dad came to see me for my birthday. It was miserable. I was homeless. While he was there, I ran off to score dope and did heroin in the hotel bathroom at night. The morning he left, we visited the Gorge Bridge a mile or so from the Mesa. It was foggy, and I was high. He knew how it would be before he came and that nothing would change with me. The obvious heroin use didn't seem to bother him anymore. Maybe he came just to show me he loved me, even if I didn't love myself. Maybe he came to show me he wasn't giving up, even if it killed him. He left me with a forced and sad smile on his face, and I returned to homeless junkiedom in Taos.

Dramas continued to unfold in Taos. I did a lot of drugs and wandered homeless and slept under a tree in a field behind McDonald's. One of my teeth abscessed, and when I had the chance to get it pulled I went to get high instead. There was a short-lived attempt to get sober at Carlos's place. By November my mom paid 400 bucks to get me a room on the second story of a white stucco building across from the jail.

My neighbor prep-cooked in the mornings and drank malt liquor at night. There was a chunky flap of cheek hanging from his jaw. He told me about being homeless as a younger man and his six-month coma after the extraction of a wisdom tooth went wrong. Doctors kept him in the coma so they could cut away the necrotizing fasciitis in his face every few hours. He lived many lives in his coma. He had been a big movie star whose last role was the voice of a baby duck in an animated film. Everyone loved him and mourned the end of his career. His eyes watered as he spoke. When my neighbor regained consciousness from the coma, his body had atrophied. He was still homeless. The doctors sowed his face back together, but it never looked right.

I always remembered the stories people told me. It seemed like they were always fascinating and bordering on the unbelievable much like my own, but maybe I remembered stories like my neighbor's because I identified with the pain. That apartment was miserable. That's where I met my girlfriend Danielle. I'll tell you about her soon.

The last time Tom and I spent time together was right when he got out of the hospital again, a year later. We had not talked for a long time, but I knew where he lived, and I knew he was in the hospital, so I moved in. I was renting the front room out to Johnny and his girlfriend who drooled on herself and always had four or five spoons on the kitchen counter with streaks of soot and the scattered pink crumbs of pills she called fast fives. One of her eyelids always stuck halfway shut, and she paused several seconds between every word.

Tom was happy to see me anyway. That was the life of a junkie, even at 75. You go to the hospital. You get out. Junkies are living in your house, and the party goes on. My girlfriend, Danielle, put the light bill in her name because Tom owed money to the company and asked us to. But when he made us mad one day I threw a big-box TV at his feet and busted the white powder all over his floor. Danielle and I turned the power off on the old man in the middle of winter to collect the deposit. It was the last time that I ever saw him, but not the last I heard.

A year later, he called me from Miami, where I suppose he died. Years after that, in the foyer of a church, a woman asked me if I had a grandfather who passed.

"He wants to tell you hello."

"You mean you talk to dead people?"

"My friends are passed over." She said, as if calling them dead was politically incorrect.

"Oh, well, I didn't know my grandfather. I don't know who it could be."

She struggled to get the deceased's name but could not come up with it.

"I'll let you know if he tells me his name. He says he loves you. He says you went through a lot together, and that you were in a bad way. He said he is proud of you, for doing so well. Very proud."

She walked back over to her table, and I forgot about her. My girlfriend and I talked. She said she thought contact with the dead was evil. I had my own opinions about how that worked and explained. The lady stood up suddenly and screamed,

"TOM!!!!! He says his name is Tom!!!!!! He loves you and, he is so, so proud of you!"

Taos 2011

Winter

The scars on my neck belong to her. Two cigarette burns, perfectly round and white, sit two inches below my ears where Frankenstein's creature had his bolts. I see them every time I shave, and they remind me of hard days in Denver, hard days with her. Danielle was her name, but she was just baby to me.

In the middle of our arguments we screamed in one another's faces. Sometimes, I cleared my throat and hocked phlegm into her eyes, and she spat back into mine. We tried to blow each other away with the spray of verbal buckshot until there was nothing left of us. Ten minutes later we made love on the bed or in the back seat of the Camry and found something or someone to rob. It was a game we played, and it was killing both of us.

The first time I met her, her boyfriend named Mike lay on the floor of the room I was renting trembling and bleeding through his pants. My drug dealers had pulled him out of her Camry on the south side of town and stabbed him in the knee for trying to go around me and deal with them directly. It didn't work out for him, thus the crying and bleeding on my floor.

"Hi."

"Hi."

"Are you Riley?"

"Yes. You must be Danielle."

"Sure am." She dropped Mike's head to put her hand out.

"Good to finally meet you." I smiled and pinched her fingers.

I was seeing a different girl at the time, a 19-year-old redhead who liked to smoke her dope and tell me she was on her way over hours before she left her house, but that morning in my room the look in Danielle's eye told me it was only a matter of time before we got together. Nevermind Mike and the redhead.

Danielle and Mike used to come over every day before three to laugh at me for nodding out and looking like Teen Wolf. She always tried to get alone with me, but we didn't hook up until after Mike started beating her again and I spent two weeks locked up, promising myself and everyone else that I would never do heroin again.

While I sat in jail, Mike took the battery out of her car and held her against her will in a trailer on the Mesa. Then he passed out one afternoon after he put the battery back in. She made her escape. Half an hour later, I called her from the payphone outside of the jail, and our reign of terror in Taos began.

A pistol-packing pot grower with a zipper for a mouth called Big Bag was making a move from out on the Mesa into town. He intended to capitalize on the isolated heroin market in

Taos. We rode with him and his leather-skinned girlfriend on the back roads down to Chimayo for ounces of heroin, and when we got back to town Danielle and I used our network of junkies to sell his dope. It wasn't a week before we ripped him off for a bunch of dope. He offered anyone in town a $50 bag for our whereabouts and left promises to murder me on her voicemail.

We shorted other junkies. They hated us. We stole merchandise and food from businesses. The owners and employees hated us. Several cops in town knew that I was driving the Camry and that I had a girlfriend. They hated us too, but we hated each other most of all.

Danielle had a monthly prescription for 90 Klonopin and an SSI check available on the first. We shot so much dope and took so many pills the first week of the month that our only friend quit hanging out with us. When her orange pill bottle quit rattling and the check was spent, anxiety wrought havoc. She left me freezing at the gas station at three in the morning while I was buying cigarettes and drove by a few times, screaming and giving me the finger for no reason. Later in the night, we went to the ER looking for meds.

Her Camry became our home. We cleaned out the ashtray at the casino for half smoked butts several times a day and listened to Depeche Mode and Seminole Wind by John Anderson. Our diet consisted entirely of Wendy's spicy chicken nuggets and Baja Blast. She made me give her a shot of dope visibly mixed with my own blood, to intentionally contract Hepatitis C. That way I could no longer use contamination as an excuse for why I wouldn't share a hit or a rinse with her. One afternoon I pulled over on the side of the highway and proposed to her with her own wooden ring made from an old long board. She said yes and we made out like two outlaws in love.

A lot of guys liked her. One of them lived in a nice apartment his parents paid for. His name was Dustin, and one afternoon, he said something about her that made me mad. Then he gave us 40 bucks to go score, so she and I split it between us and put dirt in his bag. He called to complain, but we quit answering the phone. Later that night, I decided we should sleep at his place, so I parked in his parking lot and told her,

"Get all of our blankets and meet me at the front door, baby."

As I walked through the cobblestone courtyard of the adobe apartment complex, I wondered how mad he was and thought of what I was about to do. I fingered the baggie in my pocket. At his front door breath billowed out of my mouth, and the raps of my knuckles on his door bit cold into my bones. I put my hand back into my pocket and waited. The television played on the other side of the door. He opened it, but the chain only allowed a few inches.

"Who is that? Riley? What do you want? I ought to mess you up for selling me dirt! Get out of here!" The interior light of his apartment poured out yellow through the crack in the door. It looked warm and comfortable.

"I know. I know. Listen. I got something here, to make up for it." I moved my arm and hand in my pocket, to indicate it was in my pocket. "Open up, so I can show you."

"Okay." The door closed momentarily while the chain latch came off. The knob turned. I grabbed it and lodged myself in the frame so he couldn't close the door.

"What are you doing? You can't stay here! Why does she have blankets? Dude, what the f*ck? Seriously?" A pile of blankets with Danielle's legs bounced through the courtyard towards us. I made sure she got in before I let him shut the door.

She threw the blankets on the shag rug in front of his TV. He whined in the kitchen and flapped his arms, but we disregarded him until we had settled in and I felt ready to address him. His accusations were mostly accurate, except when he said we didn't have any heroin. We did, just not for him.

After she and I situated things, I showed him the $20 bag we had. It was enough to shut him up, because we promised to share. We told him we would split it three ways, but in the bathroom, she and I split it down the middle. Afterward, we rinsed the spoon and cotton filter a few more times, until all that was left was dirt and ash in the spoon. Then we sucked it up into his syringe and came out of the bathroom to give it to him. He happily took the syringe full of dirty water and never accused us of anything until we hid ourselves in the bathroom again.

Danielle had her pants down, and I sat on the toilet applying cortisone cream to a patch of eczema on her rear end and thigh. She leaned over the sink. The door was locked while I took care of my baby.

"Open up. I know you're in there doing more! Open up! You pieces of sh*t!" The door shook as he pounded. "Open up! Open the f*cking door!" The door hit her in the head when he kicked it in.

My hands ripped the cedar towel rack out of the wall, before I could think. I beat him with the rod back out of the bathroom and side-to-side across the living room. A symphony of rage blared out of me and into my opponent. I was the impassioned composer of a brutal work, wildly conducting an orchestra of fingers, fists and arms. He tripped and fell backward over his coffee table and couch.

My shirt was off and sweat dripped. I threw the rod at his face. He could have it, because I owned him now. I leapt onto his chest for the crescendo of my opus and went to work. My legs pinned his arms to his chest and stomach. Bare knuckles bloodied themselves on his cheeks, and his face turned side to side with each punch. Snot and blood leaked from his mouth and nose, and he squealed as I stopped to catch my breath.

"Please, stop! Please! Please!" My teeth bit into my bottom lip. I looked at him for a second with my fist cocked back, before I tried to drive it through the back of his skull. His face was swollen and discolored and bloody.

"That's what you get for messing with my girl," I thought, and jumped up to grab the biggest butcher knife in the kitchen. About 10 inches of blade shined in the living room light.

"I will spill your guts on this f*cking floor! Give me your phone! Go to your f*cking room and don't come out until we leave! You hear me, mother f*cker! I will f*cking kill you!"

He didn't say anything. He gave me his phone and held his face as he walked into his room. People around town always told me that he was a fighter. Supposedly he stood up to the most feared dealer in town, Diablo, once and even "gave him a run for his money." Everyone always said he was tough, but not that night.

Danielle and I made a bed on the floor out of our blankets. She pulled up some pornography on his phone. Whatever meth we did the day before was too strong and the heroin was too weak to get us to sleep, so we had sex on and off throughout the night. Sometimes, I smoked cigarettes and tried to write poetry on pieces of cardboard box. She played dress-up with some clothes that she had brought in. Later in the night she said something that hurt my feelings, so I used the scissors in my hand to stab myself in the leg a few times. Daylight broke, and there was forgiveness and more sex. The blood on his face was crusty and black when he peaked out of his bedroom on our way out.

Taos-Denver
Winter 2011

Violent and otherwise destructive behavior was a defense mechanism, necessary to maintain a life of ruthless drug addiction in the streets. It was the unsurprising side effect of a cold and calloused heart, which had no room for things like sentimentality or love. Those things make a person weak and vulnerable in a world where dogs eat dogs, and even mothers eat their children. That may sound extreme, but that is how it was to me. That is how I saw it. If I would sell myself for drugs, plunge a blade into my stomach, steal my grandmother's jewelry or subject myself to the harsh reality of the streets day in and day out, what would stop me from doing the same to you?

Nothing.

Somewhere in her head, I was half-baby and half-bunny like her beloved Bunny O'Reilly from childhood. Her mom had inadvertently programmed her to love that name with the stuffed animal, and her father programmed her to love men that were no good to her, even though he was pretty good to her when I knew her. I fit the bill. Half-bunny and half-baby, she called me Bubby when I was capable of compassion, but when I had heroin eyes and the hiccups she just called me Clyde.

"Hey Clyde! How come you never call me Bonnie?"

"Cuz your name ain't Bonnie!"

"So what? A Clyde ain't nothing without a Bonnie. Just like you ain't nothing without me. You're my Clyde. I want to be your Bonnie."

"You are my Bonnie, baby! But, that ain't your name. You know how I am. It's like you wanting me to speak Spanish to you."

"Yeah! I want you to call me Bonnie, and I want you to speak Spanish to me!"

"What am I supposed to do? Have conversations with myself? You can't even understand it. That's weird. Like calling you Bonnie."

"So what? Call me Bonnie, Clyde! Speak Spanish to me! It's sexy!"

"Yeah right! You're name ain't Bonnie, and you don't speak Spanish! Now, drop it!"

We told everyone we were in love, but love was impossible for people like us. What we really had were attempts to fill our lives' emotional voids with each other and chemical imbalances in our brains that manifested themselves as romantic fantasy. In a very short time we became very close. Probably because we spent every second of every day together, and every day tried us.

The trajectory of my life scared people before she came around, but now it was a 20-pound cannon ball ripping through the air about to smash anyone and anything that got in its way, even her. Instead of just one, both drug dealers in town wanted to kill me. Most junkies wanted to beat me up, and at least one cop promised to send me to prison the next time she found me. But, the real reason we left Taos was that the heroin was no good since my favorite dealers got busted, and Danielle said she could make big bucks stripping in Boulder.

Eight miles north of town, heading to Colorado, a friend of ours called me up and asked if we could score for a kid who was new to Taos at the homeless shelter. We came over. The kid sniffled and his eyes watered when he yawned. He was sick for sure, so we said we would pick up some for him from one of our dealers named Joe and be right back. But we drove to Denver after we scored from Joe. Our friend called to tell us we were disgusting pieces of trash, and he was right. I imagined our departure in the grainy black and white of a 1930s movie featuring Bela Lugosi as Dracula, like we were some mad scientist's undead creatures fleeing to the hills from an angry mob of town folk wielding pitchforks and torches.

That first week in Denver is mostly a blur. Somehow, we got a hold of some speed and slunk up and down Colfax in the

Camry between Wadsworth and Federal, suspicious as they get at all hours of the morning, but the cops never bothered us for it. At a 24-hour donut shop, we took the $2 and 39 cents out of the tip jar. It must have been early in the month when her SSI check came in, because we were in and out of adult novelty shops across Denver buying all kinds of stuff and had a hotel room. We made connections with new dealers, and even let some homeless guy videotape us having sex in a hotel room one night. I stole a pair of stilettos for her, but there was something we had to take care of before she could start stripping.

 Not long before we left Taos I missed her vein with an injection and deposited the warm, dirt water of a rinse into the muscle of her forearm. She was thin. Her veins rolled a lot, and she moved around when I dug in her arm trying to register blood. The miss turned into an abscess the size of a golf ball, so we took matters into our own hands in a hotel room on Colfax.

 We stole a pack of shaving razors, a bottle of hydrogen peroxide, some gauze and tape. I broke the thin blade out of one of the shavers and snapped it in half. In the poorly lit bathroom she stood in the tub, while I knelt on the floor outside of it. Danielle shook, and her lips curled in distress. With her right wrist in my left hand I looked at her and said with a smile,

"Now baby, I know that I look like one and everything, but I feel like I should tell you that I'm not a doctor."

"Shut up! It's not funny! Now hurry up!"

I pushed the sharp side of the blade into the thin, yellowed skin on the head of her abscess. A snake of black blood and green puss slithered down her arm and thudded in clumps on the floor by the drain. She recoiled, but I held her wrist and pulled her back.

"Now, we have to squeeze it." I pinched her flesh on either side of the bleeding wound and squeezed it. More blood and puss oozed out. Her body shuddered, and she groaned curse words. We were high on heroin, but it didn't make much difference for her. It was painful. I poked a hole into the top of the bottle of peroxide and sprayed a jet of the fluid into her wound. It fizzed and foamed on the blood.

"Okay. That should be good." We wrapped the wound in gauze and taped it up and went to sleep.

The next night we went up to The Bus Stop which is a strip club in Boulder where she had worked a couple of years before. After 15 minutes of my waiting in the car, she walked out fuming and cursing back at one of the bouncers, and he screamed from across the parking lot that she was a junkie whore. They did not want her back with a bandage on her arm like that. So, we headed back to Taos.

I wasn't afraid of the death threats there, because if there was anything I knew about Taos, it was that no one's word was worth much. The people who wanted to kill me would have to find me first, and even if they did, they would have to deal with me when they did. I'm not saying that they weren't dangerous people. They were, but what I am saying is that when it came down to it, so was I.

We spent the next few days in Colorado taking advantage of the easy access to decent heroin. She and I called a guy we knew in Taos and had him send us $100 for dope we promised to bring him on our return. We broke into it right away.

Thirty minutes out of Denver a blizzard blinded us, and snow covered the interstate. The radio played. The heater warmed the car. She sat naked in the passenger seat, and my hand rested between her legs when the car spun off the road. The car did a few 360s on the highway before we slid down the embankment of the median. In two minutes a cop came to help us, so Danielle put on a jacket and rolled down the window. He told us to get off the road once he helped us get back onto it. We stopped at the rest stop a few miles up the highway and spent the night.

When we woke up, it was light and the roads were safe. I found the $10 bag of heroin we lost under the seat the night before and split it with her. It was the last of what we bought for the guy who sent us the $100 from Taos a few days before. The heroin was all gone now.

"What do you think, baby? It's a four-hour ride to Taos, and the dope's no good there."

"I know, Bubby. I know. Let's go back to Denver."

Denver
Winter 2011

I wanted to write, but what I wrote was sad and hard to understand. I scrawled in desperation like a lunatic smearing his own blood on the walls of a cave to leave a message of despair. It was a final attempt to explain the horror of losing my mind and starving to death in a pitch-black tomb.

Danielle and I threw snow on top of the sheet we used to cover the Camry in the Walmart parking lot. The wind wouldn't pick it up that way, and it covered us from potential witnesses of our naked bodies sweating and grinding and cursing and screaming at each other for more. We spent hours like that, breaking periodically, to roll down a window, lift the sheet and check to make sure the cops weren't surrounding us.

It is hard to say how long we had been awake, but several days, probably, since we had met a guy named Chivo. Maybe five days. Maybe a week. But too long. And the meth was potent on top of it. Mexican stuff, cooked in huge laboratories across the border, produced by the barrel and smuggled through tunnels to distributors like our friend Chivo. The chemicals cooked my frontal lobe and the backs of my eyeballs and incited a voracious sexual appetite in both of us.

The night dwindled away before we knew it, the way it does when the night is fun. Imminent daylight loomed somewhere over the horizon. We had an hour, maybe two before the sun came up, but we knew that we had to make plans to get our fix. Shivers and sneezing and sniffles and diarrhea were around the corner if we did not come up with something.

We thought we were in Denver after we had failed to find a place to stay in Boulder the night before. It was time to move, so we took the sheet off and drove into the unfamiliar expanse of urban sprawl.

We pulled in under the lights of a 24-hour gas station, and I sat outside on the curb. Danielle blubbered all over herself and rambled through feigned tears and dramatic sobs to patrons coming in and out of the store. She had some sad story to tell them, but no one cared. The meth and lack of sleep corroded the circuitry in our brains that helped us remember to not act like drug addicts. It wasn't long before six squad cars pulled up.

"So I'm not going to find any drugs at all in the car, if I search it right now? Are you sure?"

"Absolutely, Officer. We don't even do drugs! What is this all about? I don't understand why we are being searched." I was appalled. Danielle sat to my left on the hood of the cop car.

"Well, we got a call about you. We are doing our jobs. I'm going to search the car. Do I have permission?"

"Of course. We have nothing to hide."

"And, we won't find anything? I want to make sure. If there is anything in the car, we will find it and you'll go to jail."

"Nothing. We don't even do drugs, like I said. You can search it. Call the dogs, for all I care. There are NO DRUGS in that car, whatsoever! GO AHEAD! Waste your time if you want. I don't care."

Within 30 seconds, one officer held two syringes high above his head in the air like a proud cat with a dead mouse. Other officers continued to search the vehicle. I finally quit lying about it and took the charges for both of us. If I confessed my guilt, they would let her go to avoid paperwork. There was a chance she could get me out.

"Those are mine. Anything you find in that car is mine. She didn't know anything about it."

"Oh. Really? Are you sure about that?"

"She has nothing to do with it. She doesn't even do drugs. Those are mine, and anything else you find. She doesn't do drugs."

"She doesn't even do drugs, huh? That makes sense. A second ago, you didn't do drugs either." The officer smiled at how stupid the whole thing was, and my face admitted that it was.

"No sir." A syringe slipped out of Danielle's underwear and down her pants leg onto the pavement right in front of the cop. "That's mine, too!"

"Oh, really? That's yours too, huh?"

"Yes. Like I said, Officer, she doesn't do drugs." He smiled at me.

They hauled me off handcuffed in the back of the squad car, and she stayed with the Camry. I insisted on getting medical attention before I was booked into jail. The doctor hated junkies like me and was extremely rude. He only offered blood pressure medicine, and I called him a, "f*cking b*tch," to show my gratitude. The officer who transported me to the jail made friendly small talk. Country music twanged on the radio, and he turned it up for me. It was about 7 a.m. when he dropped me off at booking.

A lady nurse frowned as she tried to take my blood pressure and check me medically for admittance into general population.

"HOLD STILL! I'm trying to get your pressure! HOLD STILL!!!"

"I am. I am. I haven't moved a bit. What are you talking about?"

"I'm talking about you shaking like a leaf! STOP IT, NOW! I'm so tired of this, sh*t!" She finally got a decent reading and took the cuff off my arm. She sighed. "Do you want to hurt yourself? Do you feel suicidal?"

I looked her dead in the eyes. She was a rude lady. "I'm homicidal, b*tch!"

The observation tank is where potentially psychotic and suicidal inmates like I was are observed. Bright fluorescent bulbs buzzed all day and night in the cold cell. Through the large window inmates and guards of both sexes laughed at my naked body. They fed me the cold rejects of yesterday's dinner on a Styrofoam tray, so I didn't use a plastic one to beat myself to death. I had a blanket and a turtle suit, which has two Velcro straps for the shoulders and enough fabric to cover the front and hind quarters, but I was too psychotic to wear it.

When I first arrived, I was ornery and miserable and offensive as usual, coming down from a long time of not sleeping because of the meth. Sure, but not psychotic, not yet. When they put me in a cell where the lights never turned off and kept me on display like some savage beast for all to see and laugh at, I lost my mind completely. Male and female inmates pointed and laughed at my naked body standing and lost in the middle of the cell. The guards taunted me and cursed me out through the glass window every night.

My mind played terrible tricks on me. Danielle had made her way into the jail, but now I hallucinated that she was at a music festival in a park down the hall with these two elfish twins, a boy and girl. They took Ecstasy and bought McDonald's after they came down and the show was over. I watched through the feed slot in my door. Later the guards passed my girlfriend around in a broom closet like she was a rag doll. I screamed with fierce intensity for the number of hours only the mentally deranged can. I screamed till it felt like I had swallowed chunks of glass.

Then the jail turned into a garage, where Danielle got into her car with the twins. They took her from me. I screamed into where the door went into the wall. Danielle was in the room with me, talking to me, telling me she had to go with them. Then, she turned into my blanket and was gone. I screamed at the wall and door.

Two black guards ran a sex ring out of the showers. They offered the sexual services of inmates, male or female, in a steamy sauna for a decent price and threw in a fully loaded meth pipe for free. Danielle was prostituted but they kept her in a bucket of ice, until Dustin showed up. She loved Dustin. He had what she wanted. I screamed. My mattress was full of sex toys, and I tried to get them out to throw them into the hallway. When the black guard came to check on me, I pretended I was sleeping.

I had a conversation with an older Mexican gentleman, who sat on the partition between the toilet and the rest of the cell. We talked for a couple of hours at least. Mostly I talked. I looked back at him, to get a response, but there was only an empty carton of chocolate milk on the partition.

In the mirror, I found a piece of black tar heroin pressed up into the crack around it. I scraped it off with a plastic fork into a paper cup and mixed it with water. I hovered over it, on the toilet, trying to hide it from the guards. They regularly barked threats and insults through the window. After the heroin mixed sufficiently with the water, I lifted it to my face to snort it. The unmistakable stink of another person's feces filled my nostrils. I threw it away, but that's what people do in cells like that. They throw their feces at the walls and windows.

There was an emergency button on the intercom system, which I was not supposed to press. A young nurse with dark skin, black hair and blue eyes was on the other side of it. I hoped she would help me, but she told me repeatedly to stop pressing the button. "DO NOT PRESS IT AGAIN!" I pressed it again. The two black guards opened the door, "Put your hands on the wall. It's okay. We are here to help." They ripped me out of the cell by the hair and a foot and dragged my shriveled, naked body down the hall, upside down. The pretty nurse laughed.

They put me in the hole, and from inside of it I heard crazy conversations. A woman and the cops.

"Oh yeah, I told him to go to little league. You know he loves it."

"Yes, ma'am. We are sure he does. Now how are we going to drain this abscess on your arm?"

"Oh. Let me sit in the chair, or lie down on the table? I don't know. Y'all are the experts. Tommy is at little league practice. I don't want him to know about this."

"Don't worry, ma'am. We'll have you all fixed up in a minute."

Then, someone had me in their crosshairs, someone with an automatic rifle. I danced in place and screamed in the hole. If I kept my feet off the ground, they couldn't shoot me through the crack under the door. I screamed for my life, "THEY ARE GOING TO SHOOT ME!!!! HELP!!! HELP!!!! HELP!!!"

Hours of screaming passed before the voices of officers told me to get on the ground. I did. When the door opened, they asked me, "Do you see that red dot? We will tase you. Do not do anything stupid." They put me in the happy chair, which is a wheelchair without the front two wheels and an excessive number of Velcro pieces to strap lunatics down. I struggled for hours after they put me into it. I passed out from exhaustion for a few moments, before they came to tighten them again. They took me to video court, and I fell naked in front of the other inmates and screamed and cried. When they put me back in the hole, I defecated on the floor.

Eventually, they put me back in observation. Maybe 48 hours had passed. I didn't know, but something had to be done about my mental state. There were ants carrying crumbs of Percocet through the locking mechanism of the door, and I licked them off the wall like it was Coca-Cola being poured through. The guards laughed at me and mocked, "We are going to get you some share-o-win. Haw haw haw! It's not heroin but share-o-win, Chapman! Huh? How does that sound? Haw haw haw!" I found out it was a shot of liquid Valium, and I slept for the first time in a long time. When I woke up, an Asian male nurse came to give me another shot of Valium, but he wanted to shoot it into my butt cheek. I showed the crook of my arm and insisted he put it into my veins, "like a real man."

On the medical ward I slipped out of the psychotic fog. The sleep helped. They bussed me to my first court appearance, and I asked another inmate repeatedly, "So you don't think she was in the jail? They weren't passing her around like that?" He looked at me sideways. People don't visit jail like that. That's not how it works.

One of the felony charges got dropped immediately, but they followed through with the possession charge. I would have to be bailed out. Back in the jail, at night a lady with a clipboard came to see me and sat me at a table to ask me questions.

"What year is it?"

"2011." It was.

"Who is the president of the United States?"

"Obama." He was.

"Where are you?"

"Denver Orthopedic." This was the Adams County jail, not the orthopedic branch of a hospital and not Denver.

It was good enough. My mind improved with each time I slept and the food I ate and the Valium. They moved me to a cell with two other guys, and I made some phone calls. Danielle visited me on a screen.

She told me she would get me out. My parents agreed to put up the money for my bail. It took all day, but they finally let me out at almost 3 a.m. She and I had sex in the car until the next morning when we could score.

Someone sent us $40 via Western Union, and we called Chivo. It was hard to find his guy on Federal, but eventually we hooked up. I split the thick, black dope into our two syringes in a gas station bathroom. Before I walked out, I did my hit and felt a rush much stronger than I expected.

Usually an entire $40 balloon of heroin like that barely got me well, but my tolerance had dropped through the floor in jail. Walking to the door, the gas station cashier looked at me like, "Dang, boy, you are way too high," and I thought to myself, "I am way too high!" It was the last thing I remembered. Outside and into the passenger seat, I flopped out like a 170-pound dead fish. My head slapped the dashboard.

Some guy in the car parked next to us told Danielle,

"He's gonna die. You need to call the ambulance, or he's dead." She got out and finished closing the door, grabbed the dope and hid it in a dumpster behind KFC before she called 911.

It was a surprise to wake up in the back of the ambulance. "I hit you with just enough Narcan to bring you out of it. I didn't want to make you sick." Narcan (Naloxone) is what they use to counteract a heroin overdose, but when too much is administered it brings on precipitate withdrawal. "We are going to run your name and her name, to see if you have warrants, and if you don't, then we'll take you to the ER." I was in a stretcher in the back of an ambulance. It took a minute to figure things out. Our names were cleared and Danielle followed the ambulance to the hospital.

Danielle and I enjoyed our time in the ER. They wanted to keep me overnight, but I insisted they let me go. When a nurse tried to give me an IV, I screamed that I was afraid of needles, which made everyone laugh. I was still very high, and I screamed the lyrics to some rap song Danielle and I knew. "THAT BABY DON'T LOOK LIKE ME!!!! THAT BABY DON'T LOOK LIKE ME!!!" When they let me go, it was night and cold outside. I threw a fit, because we couldn't get a room at a hotel. We slept in the Walmart parking lot on Colfax and Wadsworth.

Denver
Spring 2011

We were faithful practitioners of an antique religion, the malevolent priesthood of a primitive and chemical mystery. All but vanished for decades, a vein of revival made its way up from Mexico in the early 1990s. Upon conversion, we sold all we had to follow our goddess. In back alleys and hotel rooms all around Denver, we built altars with blackened spoons, the bottom halves of aluminum cans, gnawed and looped leather belts, orange-capped needles, lighters, and empty cigarette boxes, the worn relics of our sacrament and liturgy. We cooked magical potions and conjured blissful sleep with vapors the smell of vinegar and brown sugar, kneeling before her altar and letting blood from our arms. We would have sacrificed our first born if she asked.

Heroin was life for us, and without her we were dead. Every heartbeat. Every thought. Every move. Every drop of gasoline in the car. Every cent we made. Every calorie we consumed. Every breath was devoted to the chase for more.

In Denver, four Hondurans started selling heroin and cocaine at 5 in the morning. They came like clockwork, because they got off the first bus that brought them to Civic Center Park. Besides Chivo, it was the only other means we knew to get heroin in town, and it was the only place it was available at 5 a.m. Chivo started at 8, but sickness started early. The Hondurans sold dimes, or 10 dollars' worth, in tightly wrapped balls made from cut squares of trash bag. Black was heroin. White was cocaine. They sold five for $40 as an incentive to buyers and allowed any combination.

At Walmart on Wadsworth and Colfax, we woke up before 5, sick as usual. I gathered together the random CDs in the car and went to see if one of the Hondurans in the park would trade a dime of black for them. Roger was the one we knew best, but he laughed at my offer. He seemed annoyed. He would not look at me.

We were out of luck, so we parked on Corona Street off Colfax right next to a 7-Eleven. In the car, we stretched and yawned. Our bodies ached, and the anxiety set in. We never knew where we would get it. We just had to have it. Watery snot and tears started, the sure signs of dope sickness.

"What are we going to do, Bubby?" Danielle lay back in the passenger seat.

"I don't know, baby. I'm tired. We can call Chivo and ask for another front, or we can do something, but it's too early to call Chivo. Let me chill for a minute. We'll get it. Don't worry. I don't know how but we will." She always said she liked me better when I was sick. Heroin made me extremely mean and difficult. When I was sick, I felt exposed and sensitive. Television commercials would bring tears to my eyes, and I was nice to her.

"OK, Bubby. I'm sick as sh*t." She held her stomach.

"I know, baby. Me too." I folded my arms and closed my eyes. My back and head ached. I pushed back into the driver's seat. Not two minutes passed before we heard a knock on the window.

A strange individual tried to talk to us through the closed window. Thick glasses, a shaved head, orange freckles on pale skin, a gaunt face. Maybe a man. Maybe a lesbian. I tried to tell the person to wait till we rolled the window down, but the person continued to talk. As the window lowered, I could hear he was a man.

"I need a ride out of here! Right now! I've got money! I'll pay you. I have to get out of Colorado!" He seemed genuinely desperate for our help. Through the window he flashed several bills, mostly ones and a five. It was good enough for me.

"Get in!"

Danielle had to open the door for him to crawl into the back, and we took off.

"Where do you want to go?" I didn't know where he went. There was nothing in the back seat but a pile of clothes.

"I don't know! Anywhere, out of Colorado!" His voice came from the clothes the pile of unfolded and dirty clothes under which he had buried himself.

"Well, maybe you could give us a little more direction. Like, New Mexico? Nebraska? Utah? If you pay, we'll take you anywhere you want." I remembered the condition of my release from jail. My travels were not to exceed a 150-mile radius from Adams County, but money was on the line.

"Utah. Sure. Let's go there."

Traffic halted for miles on the interstate. It was from people headed to work in Denver, so we were stuck for a while. He talked about the people chasing him. They wanted to kill him, and the cops would send him to prison. He had spent the previous night jumping fences to escape. A day or two before that, he threw away several ounces in a hotel room of the Black Hawk Casino, because he thought he was being set up. Danielle and I knew what he needed.

"Why don't you let us get you some heroin? That'll calm you down. We can get a hotel room and get some brown. Hey, what's your name anyway? If we are going to be helping you escape and partners in crime, we should know each other's' names."

"I'm Earl."

"I'm Riley. This is Danielle."

He agreed that getting heroin was a good idea, so we pulled off at the next exit, and called Chivo. We found a Motel 6, and Danielle checked into the room for us. Earl snuck in while we waited for Chivo. We never had much money to score, so Chivo's driver hurried to meet us at the gas station down the street. Out of the four $50 balloons, Earl gave us three to share, and he did so several more times, always giving us three and keeping one. It was like Christmas morning, and we were little kids.

When Danielle and I got high, we bickered and said nasty things to one another, not as a matter of any real hurt or problems we had, but like an allergic reaction to the heroin. There were two or three days in a row of us sitting in a dark, cool hotel room watching HBO high on heroin and Danielle and I squabbling. Earl spent time on his computer and whined about our fussing and fighting.

"You guys should love one another. You never know when you won't have the other one with you again." He whimpered. His life was hard, one of six boys, the youngest, and regularly raped by one of his brothers. His father hated him. In New York City, he found love with an old man named Tony, who taught him the trade of stealing fine art. They were busted together and sent to different prisons; Tony died of AIDS. I guessed. Danielle and I thought Earl turned tricks off the internet for the money he had, but we had no proof. On our third day together, he had us drop him off in the middle of nowhere between Boulder and Denver, because he did not want to hear us fight. His countenance was depressed, and he wouldn't make eye contact.

Danielle and I came back from trying to score all day at around 6:30, to find Earl outside of the room waiting for us. He got four balloons as usual, but this time he only gave us one and kept three. Then he gave us 20 bucks and sent us to Wendy's to get some dinner.

Earl lay on the floor sweaty and flaccid by the time we got back to the room. A few slaps to the face and yells of his name proved he had overdosed. Danielle shrieked and flapped her hands at her face in fear, while I ran to the bathroom and saturated a hand towel with water. When I wrung it out over his face and the water hit him he came to.

"Hey, mother f*cker, we're calling 911! You need to go to the hospital!" I didn't take his attempt at suicide personally. It was his prerogative far as I saw it, but overdosing himself in the hotel room where we slept was unacceptable.

"No! No! No! Don't call the ambulance. I'm okay. I'm okay." He begged us not to call. I listened to him, for some reason. Soon after all of it, I regretted not robbing him of all his money and sending him overdosed to the hospital. We would have been gone with his electronics and money before he got out of the hospital.

We feared that he would asphyxiate, so we made him sit up against the corner of the room on his bed while we watched TV. The blankets were around him, and Danielle and I must have given cues that I was nodding out with our conversation. His eyes were closed, but he was awake.

"See? Riley is nodding out," said Earl. Why doesn't he have to go to the hospital?"

"Shut the f*ck up, Earl. Or we will call 911 to come get your overdosing a**." It was 10:30.

"It's not fair. You are as high as I am."

"Shut the f*ck up, Earl!"

He was snoring at 1:30 when I went to sleep. "The Hangover" played mute on the TV. Danielle woke me up at 10.

"Riley. Riley. Wake up. I think he's dead."

"No, he's not dead." I opened my eyes and looked at him. I was not so sure.

"I'm pretty sure he's dead, Bubby! He looks dead!"

"No. He's not dead. Let's find a rinse before we check."

We found the bottom half of a coke can on a shelf below the TV. It had a spot of brown goo on the edge with a gray, shriveled cotton in the middle. It was all that was left of the three balloons he did the day before. I wondered how he managed to get that much tar into a syringe and inject it while we were at Wendy's. I thought he must have skin-popped it. It would have been several injections of black sludge, and if he had hit a vein the first one would have put him out.

We washed the bottom of the coke can with water and sucked it through his old cotton. It was not the clean thing to do, but we didn't care. She peed on the toilet and kept telling me he was dead while I split the syringes of slightly colored water. I denied it one more time before I hit a vein in her arm and then my own.

I walked out first and went over to his bed. I focused on his mouth and the strand of drool hanging from his chin. It was dried out and stuck there, the consistency of hair-sprayed spider web. When I put my hand on his shoulder to shake him awake, I screamed "Earl!" But he rolled over, cold and stiff. His legs never unfolded or changed position. The dried-out stalactite of drool stood upside down in the air, and his head hung off the bed. His eyes belonged on ice at the supermarket. They may as well have been a pair of yellow, lumpy grapes for all the life that they had in them.

"He's dead!" Danielle cried. I pulled him off the bed onto the floor. It only took a second for me to consider what money he might have on him and I reached into the pocket of his shorts to find a black leather wallet. There were $250 dollars, so I took the two big bills and left the $50.

Danielle called 911 like we should have the night before. She said the operator said to give him mouth-to-mouth. One look at his dead mouth and the thought of the stale air trapped in his lungs settled in my mind that I was not giving him mouth-to-mouth.

"I'm not giving him mouth-to-mouth!"

"Come on, Riley! Just try! Is he cold?"

"Not cold, but he's not warm. If you want to give him mouth-to-mouth get over here and do it. Or they can come do it, but I AM NOT doing it!"

She talked into the phone. "He's not completely cold. Is that a good thing? Is there a chance he might live?" She asked in tears and then turned to me. "She says to put your mouth on his mouth and breathe."

"Hang up!"

We gathered the syringes and cookers and balloons and threw them in the dumpster at the back of the parking lot. We stepped outside as the fire truck pulled up. They quickly gave up on trying to resuscitate Earl's dead body. One squad car pulled up, then another, and one more. A cop put up the yellow tape around the room, and they separated Danielle and me, to question us. She spoke so I could hear her, to get our stories to match up. The black cop dressed in blues flirted with her. She flirted back and told him she was a stripper. As I wrote a statement on the hot hood of a running squad car in the sun, I wondered how many years I could get for it. Would these be my last minutes of freedom, scribbling and nervous on the hood of a cop car?

An unmarked car pulled up with two detectives. They wore jackets, slacks and ties and had personality. They slicked their black hair back, true to their Hispanic heritage. One of them talked to me about the Hornets and mentioned the Nuggets. Sickly scents of pomade and cologne mixed with fear to turn my stomach. The detective's partner walked around and talked to the policemen before he walked up to me.

"Look. We got an overdose to go to right after this, two blocks away. Another dead body. We don't have time for all of this. Where are the syringes and cookers? You don't think he overdosed on air, do you? No. We don't either. Now, we understand, you and your girlfriend got scared and hid all the stuff. But we need some evidence of his drug use. We need some syringes for evidence, and we'll get you two on your way. I promise."

They took me to the dumpster where we tossed the stuff, and made me climb in, but I couldn't find it. There were several empty 20-ounce bottles from another room with syringes in them. We never put our syringes in bottles like that, but the detective seemed satisfied.

"OK. Grab a few and give them to me."

They took some pictures and got our written statements. Things wrapped up, and the coroner came. A hearse came to pick up the body. It was obvious that one of the two men working for the company with the hearse enjoyed his job, maybe too much. He wore a black three-piece suit and a felt top hat, with a gold chain to a watch in his breast pocket and a monocle. I didn't know hearses picked up overdosed bodies out of hotel rooms, but that's what I saw that day.

When they finally took the yellow police tape down and released us from the scene, Danielle jumped into my arms and wrapped her legs around my waist. We shouted in glee and relief and made out in front of the last two cops on the scene. It was over, and we were free. I still had the $200.

The first thing we did was call Chivo and met one of his guys at a gas station. When his driver showed up, I told him what happened. It didn't matter to him. They wanted the money. At some point in the day, I spilled the last of our heroin out of a cooker onto my khaki pants. She was mad, so we went to Home Depot on Quebec. I tried to steal a bunch of copper wire to scrap for money, but on the way out of the door, Loss Prevention drove me to the ground so hard the scab on my knee had fabric from my pants in it and turned green. Denver County smelled better than Adams, and they let me out after three days for petit theft.

A week later, the coroner called to ask what I knew about Earl. I told him what Earl told me; maybe it was true, maybe not, but it's what he said. His tone of voice seemed bewildered over the phone. Sometime after that, on our way to Danielle's first night at the Hustler Club, a strange figure riding a scooter on Colfax pulled up next to us. Danielle and I looked over at a lesbian in her mid-50s wearying a black leather cap and vest, thick glasses, orange freckles and pale face. Her hair was red and grey and buzzed off. Could it be Earl? It looked exactly like him. We laughed about when the 911 operator had instructed us to give him mouth-to-mouth.

I never felt much about robbing the dead man, or the fact that the last words he heard before he died were me telling him to, "shut the f*ck up." There was no time to feel bad about it, when spilled hits of heroin and three days in jail were so disappointing. The only thing I ever thought about it was that we should have robbed him when he was overdosed and called the paramedics. It would have been less trouble for us.

Denver
Summer 2011

My mother told me about one of the girls from my class had found a husband, by means of a "whirlwind romance." We hadn't talked for years, and it was so far in my past that my emotions weren't involved, but I found myself jealous of this "whirlwind romance." What did that mean anyway? Did they meet on a backpacking trip in Europe? Did he have a band of mariachis play a song up to her in a hotel balcony before he proposed? What exactly did it entail, and why didn't I ever experience one? Before long the voice in my head approached it logically, "You've done all kinds of other things, equally valuable or more than a 'whirlwind romance.'"

You see? The kind of girl I appreciated was harder and wilder than the girls I grew up around. Characteristics valued most by the girls I grew up with are things like money, family name, being Catholic, college or high school alma mater, preppy clothes, fondness for beer or having belonged to some fraternal order in college. The girls I ran with valued much different things like violence, IV drug use, robbery, rap sheets and drug dealing to name a few. So, my romantic relationships never involved making passionate love under the stars in the hills of rural Italy or lavish parties held by rich frat boys in their parents' mansions, but they did involve sharing a bag, taking hostages when necessary, shooting each other up, draining abscesses, or sometimes sweaty, stinky copulation all night long in a Toyota Camry parked outside of a convenience store. Looking back, I'm pretty sure you can use the word whirlwind somewhere in there as an adjective, just not to describe romance.

After Earl died on us, my mom paid for a room at a hostel in Boulder which was good, but our Mexicans and Hondurans worked out of Denver. We would scheme from Boulder, through Adams County and into Denver County. Five dollars of gas got us one way. More than once, we ran out of gas and rolled up to the pump where we would meet Chivo.

We planned to kick heroin often and took some heavy antipsychotics to help us sleep on one occasion. We took 400 milligrams of Seroquel a half-hour before we drove to Denver. I put my finger down my throat and threw up bile and yellow crumbs of pill before we got in the car and drove down. Danielle got mad, and I put my arm out to shield myself from the cloud of fists whirring around her head in the passenger seat. My hand broke her nose. It was an accident, but no one believes that when you're a junkie and your girlfriend's nose is black and green and broken.

I stole our neighbor's laptop out of his room while he was passed out on the floor, and I bragged about it to someone who told him. When he busted into our room with his fists clenched, I knew why he was there, but I put my hands up and acted innocent.

"Whoa! Whoa! Whoa! What are you doing, man!?! I don't want to fight! Please! I'm sorry! Please!"

He stopped a few feet in front of me and reconsidered. Did I deserve this? I might be innocent after all, but while he considered showing mercy, I tried to put my cigarette out on his eyeball. We went to the ground, and my temple hurt every time I chewed for the next week.

Danielle got a job stripping. It was at a new place, where she didn't make much money. She came home at night with $60 for however many lap dances she did and exhausted. Sometimes when she put her makeup on and got dressed, tears filled her eyes, and she would do the thing girls do to keep their makeup from running when they cry. I would push my forehead against hers, kiss her and say,

"Remember this! When you're out there and these men make you feel like a piece of meat, remember I love you. Remember that you're my girl. You're mine. I'm yours, and that's all that matters. I love you, baby!" It always cheered her up.

At the hostel, a lanky guy with black hair would come sit in a pile of our dirty clothes and watch me smoke weed while he ranted about being a pervert, his roommate and the dangerous naivete of the girls who answered his Craigslist ads. He called me and Danielle his mother and father, and she and I laughed for hours at everything he said. It was so funny, because he wasn't high. Sometime after that, we saw him on the news in Denver.

The news segment dubbed him the "Porta-Perv" because he had just been nabbed for spying on women at a yoga festival from the bottom of a Porta Potty. Apparently, a woman saw him moving down there and ran to get a security officer. He locked himself inside for a while and busted out of it to make his escape. A police officer arrested him a week later when he realized a panhandler fit the description of the "Porta-Perv."

A news article about the incident quotes him as saying,

"There's bacteria in there, but to me it's just normal... we all have bodily fluids. It seems terrible, but it didn't actually smell that bad or anything. I still would have done it even if it smelled a little weird, because where there is muck, there is gold."

The article states later that he operated a porn website and worked as a male escort using the name "Bunnyman," and insists he did it for the love, not the money. Danielle and I couldn't believe it. The guy got three years for it.

A Gallup poll named Boulder the happiest place in the U.S. at the time. It was late spring, but all we saw and wanted was in the dark dungeon of our room. We only left to score in Denver, and the sun hurt our eyes when we did. After a month, we moved back down to Denver.

Our favorite part of town had become Federal south of Colfax. It was where men pushed coolers on wheels and sold popsicles made from pineapple pulp and condensed milk. Stores sold sweet bread and piñatas, painted in pastel pink and green. Asian stores sold things we never saw before, but we still called it "Little Mexico." The people there didn't call the cops like they did in other parts of town. We attained nirvana every time we closed our eyes and baked in the car with the windows down, laid out like wet towels in the summer sun.

We walked hot asphalt in flip flops looking for receipts or cigarette butts till our feet were black. Chivo's driver brought us black tar once or twice a day, but while we were waiting for him one afternoon, a Mexican in a maroon-colored jeep asked us if we were waiting for our "*connecta*" in the parking lot. Of course, we were, and he offered us $15 balloons of what we called gunpowder dope. Sometimes Danielle and I did two balloons each and got nothing from it. Sometimes we split one, and my lips turned blue and scared her. It got to where if my lips weren't turning blue, then I wasn't happy.

One morning before the sun came up she tried to buy some dope from the guys in the park but got molested instead. When she came back and told me, I took off into the dark with a BB gun pistol we had bought at Walmart with her last check. She was my queen, and I defended her honor when I wasn't violating it myself.

Sometimes, we hustled hard or her grandmother paid for a room at the Denver West Inn on Colfax, across from Walmart, or Motel 6 up Wadsworth. One minute, I threatened to leave, and she begged me to stay. The next she was leaving and I begged her. Back and forth for days without a rest. One night I closed the door on her while she faced the wall on the bed and cried in her underwear on the bed. I sat on the hotel stoop and faced traffic. I drank the milk of rage and nursed evil thoughts. Despair pooled in my mind until it leaked out of my tear ducts. A glowing cigarette ember, slowly extinguished on the skin of my neck, provided enough physical pain to separate me from the torment. Ten minutes later I burned the other side of my neck.

Other nights, we lay sweaty and high on the bed with our eyes rolling in our heads, inches from each other's face, and whispered hot-breathed perversion into each other's mouths. It was usually violent in nature. We talked about sex slaves. Some nights I backed her into the corner and screamed in her face. When I finally fell asleep she called my parents, and my mom would tell her to leave, but she never did.

We reached the height of our ridiculousness when I jumped out of the car in downtown Denver and put all our clothes in a random shopping cart on the sidewalk. I made sure to take the stiletto pumps she used to strip in and that I stole for her when we first got to Denver.

"GIVE ME YOUR STILLETOS! YOU DON'T DESERVE THOSE! I'M A GIVE THEM TO MY NEW WOMAN! SHE'LL DESERVE THEM! YOU CAN FORGET ABOUT THESE!"

"HA HA! YOU THINK I CARE ABOUT THOSE THINGS? TAKE 'EM! DON'T MATTER TO ME, PUNK!"

"GOOD! AND YOU CAN FORGET ABOUT ME TOO!"

She took off. I pushed the shopping cart down the street bawling for a while before I called my little sister in New Orleans and asked her to call Danielle for me. She did and helped us forgive each other. We were addicted to the feelings of breaking up and making up like that. It was just something for us to feel.

On my 25th birthday, July 26, my mother sent $100, and we met Chivo's driver at the Burger King on 38th and Pecos. It was right after my felony charges from the night I got arrested and went crazy in jail. I ended up with one misdemeanor and had a month to check into probation. We did our hits in the parking lot. Right after I pushed off, a gun in my face and an officer's voice threatened my life. The cops took us to jail and let me out after two days. She took the charges. The cops kept the car.

For nine days I walked up and down the 16th street mall and slept in the park by the jail downtown. My ankle hurt, and I walked without my shoes on sometimes. I called my parents collect. Instead of my name, I left the number to the pay phone so they could call back and told my dad that I would check myself into jail. Day after day I wanted to, but when they let her out with misdemeanor probation, we were right back to it. Only now, we were on foot. At the McDonald's 16th, she said she wanted to stay sober.

We hooked up with a prostitute she knew from jail and did our first hits on the side of a dumpster that morning. Soon we were in a hotel room, shooting meth and sweating while Danielle and the girl turned tricks for men off the internet. I called the prostitute hatchet face behind her back, and when she was nodded out, I stole 60 bucks out of her purse. After that Danielle went with some Mexicans we knew and got passed around at their house like a piece of meat. When she came back the next morning with balloons of heroin and out of her mind from the trauma and the drugs they gave her, I took it all from her and did the drugs.

We fled from our charges in Colorado to her family in Ohio and stayed in a hotel room where it all ended. We became subjects of a criminal investigation in Cincinnati and upgraded our stay at the Sharonville Econo Lodge to the SWAT team extraction special. The last time I saw her in real life she held her hand up to the visitation window of the Warren County Jail and cried over the receiver. Her dad paid me $60 to leave their lives on a Greyhound and never come back. They had to book and release me, but I found out later that they had interrogated her while I rode that bus 84 hours back to San Francisco and a baseball-sized abscess formed on my left butt cheek. To this day I am still wanted by Adams County, Colorado, for not complying with the terms of my misdemeanor probation.

As I write this I have bad news to tell. Danielle moved on after me, and we talked over the years. We always enjoyed reminiscing about how we used to eat Wendy's spicy chicken nuggets and drink Baja Blast from Taco Bell and smoke Newport Reds, but when she met her husband, it became more difficult to talk. He was very jealous and rightfully so. They had a kid together. He was violent and in and out of prison. She struggled with chemicals and her mental health. The last time I talked to her, she had just gotten out of the hospital after a late-term miscarriage and told me she was in the process of finally divorcing her husband. Her mom had taken her son away from her, but she said she wanted to be a mother again and was done with all of the stupidity with her husband and drugs. It was difficult to understand her ramblings over the phone. She asked me to pray for her, and I did.

Danielle legally filed for divorce from her husband. She invited him over the next night to get high, and he brought over a $20 bag of fentanyl-laced heroin. He injected it into her arm, the way I did years ago, but this time, she never woke up. Danielle leaves behind two brothers, her father, her mother and stepfather and a 4-year-old son.

Portland

Winter 2011-2012

Rabies concentrates itself in the saliva and nervous system of its hosts, thereby causing its hosts to infect others with the virus through biting. Interestingly, it seems to have an intelligent strategy in spreading itself from its hosts to others. The facts associated with different kinds of super bugs, hemorrhagic fever and even the disproportionate number of white women from the states of Texas and California having Morgellon's disease fascinate me. Recreational research of diseases can be fun, but first-hand experiences with them are not. I have had Hepatitis C, multiple abscesses, infected deep-vein thrombosis, cellulitis in my arm and once what may have been sarcoptic mange, but the worst disease I ever had was my own self. It was even worse than the time I got MRSA in my spine and it almost paralyzed me.

When Angie, Cade (junkie friend's I made after Cincinnati) and I got off the bus in Portland from San Francisco we scored three $20 balloons of heroin first thing from a guy outside of Powell's bookstore. It was Saturday night, and drunken college students littered the sidewalks outside of the bars in the night. Cigarette smoke and slurred conversation filled the air and came from people who had no idea what life was like for my kind. They would go back to their beds in their apartments after spending $100 at the bar. I would sleep on the cold concrete in one of the doorways down the street with my head inches from the puddles they would tromp their stylish leather shoes through on the way home.

We all split up, and I lost my piece of heroin in a Pita Pit bathroom. The bars had closed when I found Cade and tried to sleep on the pavement next to him. Unlike Frisco we did not know the ins and outs of homelessness in Portland. We had played like kids on a jungle gym in San Francisco but didn't know where to find cardboard to sleep on in Portland.

Angie found us in the morning, and we got high one more time before we parted ways for good. I lived at the Joyce while my parents paid the rent, because I promised them that I was taking every possible step to get into a place called Hooper detox. Truthfully, I had never been there or called, and I wasn't taking any steps to get in.

I paid 50-something dollars a night, but I told them it cost $80 and used the extra to buy heroin. The dive from paying $20 for 300 milligrams of morphine on pill hill in San Francisco's Tenderloin to the $20 mouse turds of mediocre heroin I bought from the guy on the third floor of the Joyce was hard to stomach. It never gave me what I wanted, and I was sick by 4 every morning. I did a lot of rinses to pass the time and injected some ashy water in my forearm one afternoon.

That night I got cotton fever. It started like always with sweaty chills and severe bone and muscle aches. My head pounded and the shakes steadily grew, along with a kidney pain. The shakes turned into jerking convulsions and lifted me off the bed like Linda Blair in 'The Exorcist." I puked on the floor and sheets. My mouth and throat got so parched my lips stuck together. I cried for water. I tried to drink and retched it all back up a second later. I puked and pooped in the common shower down the hall. My head and kidneys hurt so bad I cried and puked some more. I did not sleep. "At least Ebola kills you," I thought to myself as the sun came up. CNN showed Gaddafi bloodied and beaten by his enemies. He had been captured in Libya.

My parents sent the money for another day and the dealer had to make change in his room after he gave me the $20 balloon. While I cooked up my hit, a pebbly slime rose in my chest, and I almost peed in my pants. I grabbed the small trashcan to pee into and puked into it simultaneously. A large squirt of diarrhea ran down my leg, and it took a second to collect myself, before I did the shot. On my way to the shower, my dealer met me in the hallway with the $60 for rent and cigarettes.

After the shower, I watched TV for a while and tried to relax. My kidneys and head ached still. When I went to pay rent at the front desk I realized that I had left the money in the bathroom. It was gone, and I told management that I had to go pick up another Western Union at Safeway. My dad yelled at me over the phone about having to send more money.

I wore the only thing in my room that wasn't plastered with excrement, a pair of pajama pants completely ripped from the crotch and down the leg, and no underwear. It was cold and the 10 blocks to Safeway were embarrassing while I tried to keep from exposing my private parts on the street. I waited two hours for the money, but when I returned to the Joyce management kicked me out for finding a syringe under my bed and the smell coming out of the trashcan. They seemed to think that I was defecating in it.

The front desk clerk, an inadequate type with thick-rimmed glasses, a skinny neck and a buzz cut, told me about finding an overdosed body in one of the rooms last week and gave me a pair of jeans that were too small. I bought some animal cookies in the vending machine. The pink and white frosting on them provoked my guts into gurgling while I listened. Perhaps the treat was a bit premature.

For the next three mornings, I walked to the MAX rail in the dark and took the red line to the Rose Quarter. Being new to Portland, it seemed an amazing place to live. It was progressive and of a size somewhere between a town and a city. It boasted one of the top public transit systems in the nation. Everyone bought their milk and eggs from the farmer's markets and rode retro fixed-gear bikes with skinny tires and smoked weed wearing hipster glasses. However, cool a place Portland was to live, I still slept outside, and it would never be that cool for me.

But at least I was finally fulfilling my promise to my parents about trying to get into the detox.

I slept in an asphalt parking lot with a jacket over my legs through the cold nights. Hooper took me in on the third morning, but the day before that, my arm turned into a thick piece of firewood, hard and swollen. It was excruciating. The ER at Good Samaritan Hospital on 23rd told me it was cellulitis. When I first got there the doctors and nurses sneered at the smell in the room. Fish scales of hardened dead skin covered the soles of my feet from the black and white Adidas I found in San Francisco and had worn for weeks without socks.

The medical detox at Hooper was easy for me, except that no amount of washing my feet helped. It became an unsettling stench that started light, but the longer I sat in any one place, everyone had to ask, "What is that smell? Whoa! What is that?" I watched movies, ate Graham crackers and drank milk, until they gave out the sleeping aid Trazodone at 8 p.m. They put me in a bed next to a guy with teeth like broken glass and ever-present earplugs in his ears, like people do in jails. It made me think he had a condition that caused his brains to leak out of his ears and that the piece of pink foam acted as the drain stop. After seven days I took my last two milligrams of buprenorphine and left a few days later for a sober living facility called the 8x8.

Men and women who had struggled with addiction or alcoholism lived in the tiny rooms of the 8x8. Each room had a kitchenette and toilet. The city paid our rent as long as we attended five AA meetings a week and stayed sober. I lived on the sixth floor, and all but one girl on the floor had already relapsed. In the lobby, another tenant told me about the Sunday night men's meeting in the conference room attached to the lobby. She said it was a place where men got real with themselves and serious healing took place. I never went, because I had been sick for so long I didn't know how or even want to be anything else. Healing scared me.

My first two weeks there something in my spine hurt like I never hurt before, and I took 24 IBPROFENS every six hours to sleep. My stomach bled inside from the pills, and everyone said that I should go to the ER. I refused to go but moaned and wailed loudly every night in the lobby of the 8x8. The black lady who worked the front desk at night couldn't stand it or me for that matter. It was easily the worst pain of my entire life, and when my mom came to visit me on Thanksgiving Day, she said,

"No one's face looks like yours does that doesn't need to go to the hospital."

We took a taxi to Good Samaritan to see what they said. It was my idea that after the CT scan I would go smoke a cigarette, but the doctor said,

"You have at least two infected discs in your back, and it looks like some vertebral osteomyelitis. That's infected bone. We'll get you up to a room as soon as we can and start a round of antibiotics now. I was going to give you some dilaudid, but your mother says you're a recovering addict, so we'll stick with Percocet, 10 milligrams every six hours."

"Um. So, can I go smoke now?"

"No. I'm sorry."

I needed a cigarette. Ten milligrams of Percocet every five minutes couldn't touch my tolerance for the pain. My back hurt, and I thought my mom should have minded her own business.

"Well, Mama, you know what I think, right?"

"No. What do you think, Riley?"

"F*ck this sh*t show is what the f*ck I think! Just a bunch of stupid mother f*ckers around here!" I reminded myself of Turtle Tom. He lived in horrific pain. The doctor shrugged before she walked out of the room.

On the third floor of the hospital my mom brought me Thai food and several bottles of IBUPROFEN, but the doctors discovered the pills and took them from me. They said 4,800 milligrams every six hours was not good for me, even if it was the only thing that worked. Later that night I chased my mom out of the room, slammed the door and threw my dinner tray on the floor, so the doctors wrote me an order for three milligrams of liquid morphine. It didn't work, and they seemed surprised I wasn't more thankful.

The next afternoon I got an EKG to see if I had vegetative growths on my heart valves, otherwise known as endocarditis. If I did, things were worse than I could imagine, but while the tech and his helper ran a piece of cold metal through the slime on my chest, one of my friends from the 8x8 showed up with some heroin. I demanded to use the bathroom, and after a minute I pulled my friend into the bathroom in front of the technicians and locked the door. We took 15 minutes to fix, so the nurse knocked and made me "COME OUT OF THERE, NOW!"

At 1 a.m. a few days later my legs tingled and quit working so well. I couldn't use the bathroom, so a middle-aged blond woman came in and gave me a catheter. The night doctor ordered another MRI. I could not move my feet an inch by the time they rolled me down the hall. My blood pressure skyrocketed, and in the morning my regular doctors came to see me. The Asian one asked me if I thought four milligrams of dilaudid would be enough, or if I wanted more. To make my point about not drug- seeking I asked for two milligrams, and I cried.

I told the anesthesiologist in the OR that I had never had surgery before. Now they would remove an abscess crushing my spine.

"Well, you'll be fine, sweetie. Can you count from 100 backward for me?"

"100...99...98...97...96..."

I woke up to feel the warmth of the fentanyl evaporating and sweaty desperation forming on my brow. There were new pains in my back from where the surgeon HAD laid open the meat and used power tools to cut into my vertebrae and sowed a seam of fishing line through the skin over my spine. A pretty X-ray tech slid a cold metal case behind me shortly after I woke up, and I screamed. Different nurses brought me dilaudid and morphine every few hours. After five days of sleepy agony, I slid out of bed and used my walker and arms to get my first shower, with my mom's help.

Before I left a lady used a sonogram to run a thin rubber tube called a PICC line through a vein in my arm into my heart. It was painless, and I was never supposed to mess with it for fear of infection or ITS affecting my heart. A mesh band held the capped nozzle against the skin of my upper arm.

A week after the surgery my mother helped move me into an assisted living facility.

I shuffled with my walker everywhere I went. It took me 15 days before I could walk unassisted, and my toes only tripped me up occasionally. 23 days after surgery I had my first bowel movement and had not gone for several days before the operation. The resident doctor at the retirement home stopped in to see me. He asked me how I was coming off the dilaudid and when my last dose was.

"Um. I think yesterday morning. I think I feel okay. You know? I mean the doctor at the hospital told me that a lot of people think childbirth or kidney stones are the most painful things a person can go through, but she said that's because epidural abscesses are so rare."

"I can't imagine what that's like, but you say you feel okay for now without the dilaudid?"

"Yeah, Doc. I'm feeling okay."

"Good. Well I'm going to get a drug test from you. Let the nurse know when you are ready to pee."

The surprise of a drug test made me paranoid, so I saved some pee in a bottle in case they ever gave me another one. It was more boring and comfortable in the retirement home than ON the streets, but it was as sad. The eerie stink and dread of leather-skinned shadows leaked into the hallway while they waited for death in their rooms. Straight-faced families stared at the floor and sat around the grey skeleton of their grandfather in bed, his mouth open, his eyes absent, a tangle of tubes and wires running from him to softly beeping machines. The swollen-eyed nurses lost two or three patients a week.

The retirement home wanted to send me home after six weeks of antibiotics, but I wasn't ready to give up my handy PICC line or hospital bed or cable TV or the morphine I got, so I demanded that they send me back to Good Samaritan for an MRI. The results showed that my spine had only deteriorated since I arrived at the facility, and the doctor wrote me orders for six milligrams of dilaudid every four hours, upped my morphine and added Ativan as needed.

An old, orange lady who I called Garfield and a young African immigrant took care of my meds, and I kept them under my tongue until I got back to my room, where I administered them to myself through my PICC line. Whenever I took a shower I used a plastic card to try scraping the crocodile skin on the bottoms of my feet from the pair of shoes that made them smell so bad at the detox. At night I snuck out of my window and walked down to a trailer park to buy meth or heroin.

My nurses all knew I was high but couldn't figure out how I got it, and the administrators gave me a drug test when the maid found blackened spoons in my bathroom. When they gave me the cup, I used the old urine I saved from before. One of the administrators came to see me the next day.

"So, Mr. Chapman, when those results come back from the lab, you'll be out of here." Her tone conveyed disgust and rejoicing at the prospect of my expulsion. I was on my second round of antibiotics after the first ones didn't work.

"Okay. Well, aren't you sending the urine to a lab?"

"Yes."

"So, you'll know what's in my system, right? You'll be able to know if it was heroin or morphine, right?"

"Exactly. We'll know you were doing heroin and you'll be gone."

"No. I won't."

"Yes, you will, and then you'll probably die of the infection. Do you have anything to say for yourself, after throwing away your life like this?"

"Yeah, I do. Get the f*ck out of my room and leave me the f*ck alone until you have those results! I'm trying to watch my cartoons!"

She didn't have a response, but she left. I got caught smoking cigarettes in my room at night by one of the nursing assistants, but got away with it. Joints were harder to smoke, but I smoked them in the room too. They knew I used my PICC line to inject my painkillers, because it ballooned out where I clogged it and had to be replaced. All but one of the nurses hated my guts and wanted to get rid of me. The one who didn't hate me spent extra time in my room watching Comedy Central and went to the store to buy me every flavor of Laffy Taffy. She talked to me about sex with her boyfriend and how he didn't love her like she loved him. When she lingered awkwardly to talk to me other nurses would make up reasons to come into the room and check my charts or IV pump.

Back home my family expected me to die, so my father visited to boost my spirits and maybe spend some of our last time together. I didn't know that's what they thought, but my father had concluded from everything he heard that I would be lucky to live. He brought a carnival king cake from New Orleans for the nurses. At Buffalo Wild Wings we split a six-piece of wings and an appetizer of spinach dip, which was different. I always ate a lot of food and quickly, but the regimen of dilaudid and morphine and the hospital bed suppressed my appetite. My stomach had shrunk so that I could barely eat, and my dad attributed my lethargy and lightheadedness to anemia. He made me get my hair cut and beard shaved off. When I got back to the home, an older nurse said, "Boy! You got me all turned on, and I'm black!"

Once he got back home, he told me over the phone what tests to make the doctors run and what numbers were good or acceptable and what was bad. We paid close attention to my erythrocyte sedimentation rate, which detects inflamation and felt relieved when it went down. My father saved my life for the umpteenth time, and after three months they let me go with an envelope of 12 dilaudid and a few prescriptions to be filled in New Orleans.

I gave the nurses one last headache when I snuck out of the facility with my PICC line in. One nurse wanted to take it out, but I told her the next nurse on shift would. When the next nurse came on I told her the one before had already taken it out, and I left in a hurry. The muscles burned in my atrophied body, and I wheezed all the way to the bus stop. If there was ever an appropriate time to refrain from smoking cigarettes this was it, but I smoked at least three Camel 99s before I made it four blocks to the bus stop. In the airport bathroom, I mixed up 24 milligrams of dilaudid and pushed it down my PICC line, but my body only tingled for a second. Then I felt nothing but sober.

Between flights my dad called me.

"Seems they have a big brouhaha over at the old folks' home you were living in."

"Really? How do you know that?"

"Well, they called us, pretty frantic. Did you get out of there with your PICC line in?"

"Yeah. I still have it in."

"Sh*t! Riley!"

"It's okay. I'll take it out myself."

"I don't know about that. I think that's dangerous. Let's figure it out when you get here."

"Okay. Sounds good. We're about to take off." I walked to the aircraft's bathroom, and it moved in my heart and through my chest as I pulled two feet of thin tubing out of my arm. It was probably a biohazard, and I thought about that before disposing of it in the waste bin.

My luggage got lost, but a man delivered it all by three a.m. There were a few morphine pills in my bags, so I took them as soon as my stuff showed up. In the morning my mom took me to get my dilaudid prescription filled, but since it was from Oregon they would only fill the morphine and Ativan, no dilaudid. I refused to get the morphine filled as some sort of self-destructive protest but insisted on the Ativan. An old roach from one of my parents' parties gave me a buzz before my sisters took me to eat lunch at Frankie and Johnny's.

My sisters kept looking down and putting their hands over their eyes when I talked to the waitress. They said, "Come on, Riley! Stop!"

They found my attitude and tone appalling. The younger one laughed at the effects of marijuana on my eyes mixed with the onset of severe opiate withdrawal on the rest of my body, slowly turning me into a broken slinky. At the house, my sisters tried to watch "Bridesmaids" with me, but I passed out during the part where they got food poisoning.

I woke up in the bed on the third floor, and I thought I must have showered with my clothes on and gotten right into bed at some point in the night and forgotten about it. My sheets were dripping wet. I dreamed of swimming. Streaks of brown lined the white tile in the bathroom by the toilet, but I didn't remember getting up. I snuck downstairs and stole $14 out of my mom's purse and her car keys. I guzzled half a bottle of red cough syrup even though I knew it wouldn't do anything for me.

Over by the graveyards on Adams St. I found a crackhead lady who said she could help me get some heroin for $14. At the Chevron on Willow and Carrollton the crackhead jumped out to see if she could get me some brown for 14 bucks. The guys in the car had some but they wanted $40. She told me to drive to a few other places in "Pigeon Town" and jumped out to check at different houses. I swerved to one last house by Leonidas, and while she was in the house my guts shook. My sphincter quivered. An untied leather boot turned itself around inside of me and tried to push itself through my throat before I puked up bile and red cough syrup all over the interior of my mother's Mercedes Benz. I opened the door and slid out of the vehicle into the street to pull down my pants. An aerosol of liquid sprayed the pavement and the backs of my shoes. A trickle ran down my legs, and before the sun came up my vomit gushed onto the pavement in the middle of the ghetto. This went on for a few minutes before I gave up on the woman coming back and left. She could have the 14 bucks.

I continued to vomit on myself and let my bowels go on the drive home. "I'm going to die. I'm going to die," I repeated to myself between retching and the expulsion of bile from my mouth. Warm liquid spread across the seat of my pants.

My father met me at the front door. He knew I had stolen the car and some money, but most of all he knew I was going to die from this sickness if I didn't get to the hospital. My mother drove, and my father sat with me in the back seat. They wheeled me to the ER, where I talked the doctor into giving me some water. My dad told her not to give me any, and I puked it up like he said I would. Soon I was on the gurney in convulsions, in and out of consciousness.

"I'm about to sh*t!" I managed to gurgle to my dad and the orderly through the vomit. The orderly and my dad hooked the back of my knees with their arms and pulled me up to slide the bedpan under me.

A doctor came in and belittled me for letting them put me on so much medicine in Portland. I would have cursed him out, but it was too hard to talk and puke and convulse at the same time. He wrote an order for some dilaudid to abate the vomiting and diarrhea until I could get enough fluids to not die. I had only been home for 36 hours, but I had already stolen my mom's car, 14 bucks from her purse, drunk a half-bottle of cough syrup, puked it up all over the interior of her Mercedes Benz, defecated on the seats, tried to score drugs in the ghetto and was currently puking and pooping to death on a gurney at seven in the morning. This was exactly why I had not been home for the last three years.

When I was three years old, they took me off the bottle. My parents had a ceremony for it. They lit them all on fire and let them burn on the levee for me to see. No one ever asked me if I was ready to make that transition, and my time at the nursing home in Portland awoke a latent fantasy to return to that time. Instead of a nipple on my bottle and a liquid diet, I had thick mixtures of painkillers and the nozzle of my PICC line.

I barely got out of bed for three months. Now the dream was over, and it almost killed me. My father kept offering to buy me gum.

"Your mouth is hanging open. Gum will help you keep it closed, strengthen your jaw. You look weak." And I was.

They let me out before I ever had a solid stool, which my dad said was wrong, and the following week I went up to Baton Rouge to visit my father's mother, Turkey. I had gotten a hold of some 30-milligram oxycodones. I needed money, so I set up a visit with Turkey. He took me to eat at Popeyes. It had been over three years since I had seen him, since I lived on Octavia and Fountainbleau. His bottom eyelids hung loose from his eyeballs, and he used a cane. He was much older than I had ever known him to be. I asked him for money, and he asked me why I needed it. We both knew I was lying, but he gave me a few bucks before he left.

My parents could only have me home for a few weeks before they insisted that I enter a year-long rehab called Bridge House. It was free and boasted an extremely high success rate among its graduates. I told my parents that I wasn't using, even though I would disappear for hours and get caught lying about where I was. My sister caught me bouncing (falling asleep while standing and waking up 40-50 times a minute) one night. Soon after that I shared a needle at one of the gas stations on Claiborne with a random while Seals and Croft played on the radio and beads of sweat rolled down my cheeks. Summer breeze makes me feel fine, blowing through the jasmine in my mind.

I knew I contracted HIV from the needle and went into Bridge House a few days later. In one week I smoked my carton of Camel filters and got caught up in some commotion involving a guy called Long Beach who was threatening to stab another client with a pair of scissors. We took off together. A few days later my mom bought me a ticket back to Portland. I don't know what they thought I would do there, but at least I would be far away.

Portland

Spring-Summer 2012

Sometimes I sat on the park block benches in a cold, gray drizzle. A stranger might hand me a grease-stained box half-filled with some unidentifiable sludge and a chunk of what was alleged to be chicken breast, or I might beat out the last bit of peach yogurt onto my blackened palm before licking it up, unashamed and starving for passersby to see.

Other times I had spells of deja vu like I had seen these very same things in the same order in a dream a long time ago, or maybe it was the effect of living the same reality over and over again as the universe exploded out of nothing and created everything before it imploded in on itself and did it again.

One time I sat back after dinner in a soup kitchen, and tears streamed down the faces of two girls singing worship songs at the homeless shelter. They sang, "You give and take away. You give and take away." The theology struck me as odd, but I appreciated the passion before their friend came out to give his testimony about being a depressed teenager who found life and joy in Jesus Christ. I thought that sounded nice but didn't apply to me. There were holes in my arms that had to be filled, and I regarded nothing as sacred.

Another time I met a 54-year-old woman named Lonna squatting against a wall next to me out of the rain and smoking a cigarette. She wore funeral-parlor perfume that seemed to be mingled with the aromas of mental illness and mildew. Her mascara ran in the rain, and flecks of red lipstick stuck to her teeth. She bit her cigarette. She punched me in the shoulder. She pointed her finger.

"Look at that!" A dramatic scene unfolded 60 feet from where we crouched in the grocery store parking lot. EMTs rolled a blue-lipped and gray-faced person in a gurney out of Fred Meyer's and into the back of the ambulance. I couldn't tell if the person was a man or a woman. I just knew the person was ugly.

"Who's that?"

"Jerianne. I guess she's not coming back to the apartment with me this afternoon. Bahaha. Screwed it up? Didn't ya, Jerianne? She always does!" She threw the rest of her cigarette into a puddle. "You wanna come home with me?"

We walked west on Burnside a few blocks and took a left up a steep hill to her apartment, where she told me about how perverted the attendant at the corner gas station was and then let me crawl all over her in the dark. Afterwards we smoked cigarettes and talked in bed.

"My son died four years ago in a car accident on the coast in Washington. He was everything to me. He was all I had. I tried to kill myself last month with my methadone and klonopin but it didn't work. I took my whole months' worth of methadone and my klonopin too, but I woke up in the morning. The doctors filled my scripts again but now I have to take classes three days a week for the nine more months, and I still wish I was dead."

That's life. One morning you're on your knees kissing your pregnant wife's belly and buying diapers and rolling out pink paint on the walls of the room with the crib for the baby girl you'll be bringing home any day now, but the next morning you're on your knees in a hospital waiting room clutching your face and screaming with blood on your shirt and trying to understand why. It happens. People lose their most precious relationships in an instant, and there's nothing they can do about it but die themselves. Lonna chose a slow death and hurt all along the way.

We rented movies from the library and watched them over and over without ever knowing what they were about, because we snored through them. Anything filmed in the early '90s evoked strong feelings for me, because they were from when I was a kid, before the hatred had consummated within. I dreamed of living the life of one of the unnamed extras and disappearing into the background of the second "Lethal Weapon" movie or "Backdraft," where life was of no consequence. It was not uncommon for her to wake up with large holes burned into her sheets from nodding out with lit cigarettes.

"Did I set my bed on fire last night? I think I remember that! Ha ha! Yeah. Now I remember. I woke up and the sheets were on fire. There was a fire last night! Yup. Sure was. Jeesh! You'd think that I'd remember something like that. Ha ha! Almost burned myself up in a fire and the whole building too. Ha ha!"

In the daytime, she helped me boost merchandise from stores, but I was good at it without her. I strategized to either be in and out as quickly as possible, or if I thought a secret shopper was following me, I would walk from one side of the store up an aisle back to the other side, and down another aisle, and back up it. If anyone followed me for all of that, I would ask him why he was following me. They never knew what to say. If one was on the phone, I would ask him to say hello to his mother for me. If one was in the health-food section, I asked what a tub of lard like him was doing buying raw organic almonds. Sometimes, I would fill a hand basket and get their attention by walking toward the door and dropping it, right before I walked out. Then, while they put the items back or talked to each other about it in the room full of monitors, I would walk back through the store and steal what I wanted. Lonna kept lookout, and I filled my bags with DVDs and walked out with my arms full of merchandise and the alarms going off.

She kicked me out one morning after I nodded out on the couch all night. A few days after that I got high on meth and texted her from under a dumpster about her naked 54-year-old body and what I wanted to do it. Every day for weeks she forwarded the explicit messages along with her own haranguing texts to my mother. My mom told me that Lonna sent 28 texts before noon on a Tuesday once, and none of them made any sense.

In late May I found a cup of cold coffee in a trashcan downtown and threw it on her. She called the cops and tried to tell them I was a thief, which they already knew but couldn't take me to jail for. It was in Pioneer Square, where I used to sit and wait for licks or plant my feet in one spot with straight legs and fold at the waist like a taco trying to touch my nose to my big toe while drooling. People always stopped and woke me up to ask if I was okay or if I needed some help. I was doing great.

I moved to Vancouver, Washington, for work after that. Someone told me about the day-labor company there. It was good for 50 bucks a day, so I came to Portland at night to pick up dope after work and slept under the awning of a nail salon across the street from the day labor place. And at four I woke up to catch rides with the crew out to the landfill where we worked. The guy who drove had the aura of a potato. He wore a leather jacket. He drove a truck. He grew a bushy beard. He mumbled something about alimony payments and a daughter on our cigarette break once, but when I pictured him going home to his sad life, he was a potato, a soft, lumpy potato crying on his pillow.

After a few weeks, the company we were working for fired me for stealing other people's lunches and sleeping in the bushes while on the clock, but I tried to make life in Vancouver work anyway. I didn't give up until the incident in which a local Army veteran paid me $5 and a 99-cent cheeseburger to deposit a certain bodily fluid on a lacy pair of panties in a graveyard. Then I moved back to Portland.

On a Saturday night, a stumbling and drunk Mexican flashed the money in his wallet at me on Third by Voodoo doughnuts. He wanted me to be his date or sex or something, but it ended up that he spent about five minutes licking the side of my face while I got his wallet out of his back pocket and took the money. It was a $200 come-up, and I skipped around town until I pulled my money out to buy crack from a big group of black men in Chinatown. They jumped me badly and robbed me.

As Sunday morning broke the splatter of cold rain on the sidewalk soaked into my newspaper blankets under a Chinatown stoop. I couldn't sleep, and the loss of the 200 dollars was my only thought. My leg and hip hurt from getting jumped. It had been such a happy moment to have that money in my pocket for the morning, but I called one of my dealers anyway and appealed to her compassion. She told me to come see her in an apartment downtown where she was getting tattooed.

In the room, Dreezy and her 19-year-old girlfriend lay face down to get lace tattooed down the back of their legs. It was an ordeal, and they squirmed and squealed. The lady whose place it was kept talking to her dead girlfriend like she was floating in the room with us, and their tattoo artist asked if he should start a mobile tattoo business even though it was illegal.

Dreezy gave me a hit to hold me over, and we hung out for a while before I left.

Dreezy's haircut let you know she didn't care what you thought. There was no guard on the clippers when she ran them back over her ears without a mirror and left the tuft of blond hair on top. She had more bag under her eyes than cheek and those deep creases circled down her face and back up to her brown eyes as testimony to her life of suffering and loss. She only had half of her top teeth and sold drugs from her queen-sized bed bare-breasted in dirty cotton underwear. A stretchmark ran jagged like a bolt of lightning through the doughy abdomen hanging over the elastic waistband of her stained panties.

The state took her daughter a year before I met her, and she had a son with her brother who was taken long before that. She told me about being molested as a child like she missed it. There was nothing she wasn't into. Dreezy mentioned her affinity for bestiality once, particularly canines, and boasted of her videotaped endeavors. Before I tried to rob her, I fell in love.

I bought from her a lot, because she was reliable and always holding and generous. She fronted or gave me dope, because she liked me. It wasn't long after we met that I came to see her at her hotel room on Mcloughlin to find her jerking around her room collecting some belongings in a bag and sweating in a curly blonde wig.

"Here you go. Can you watch my place for me? Some f*cking scumbag tried to rob me earlier. I need someone here if he tries to come back." She handed me a few chunks of heroin and meth. Maybe she had reason to think the place was about to get raided and wouldn't mind if I took the fall.

"Yeah, I can watch the place."

"I don't know why, but I trust you. I'll be back tomorrow." Her girlfriend wasn't around. She was with a guy, and they took off in a truck. Later, Dreezy used this incident to make me feel special and said,

"I never trust people like that, but I knew you were different from the start."

It took her a day or so to come back, and we got close when she did. Dreezy chased her girlfriend off for being paranoid and jealous before she moved on to the next fling. I texted Danielle back in Cincinatti even though she was with another guy, and I complained about my heartache to Dreezy. Dreezy asked me if I thought she liked to hear about Danielle.

    Dreezy would finally fall asleep at around 4 a.m. Sometimes earlier, but when she was out she could not be woken up. Slapping her didn't work. Screaming was useless. We never tried pouring cold water, but it seemed doubtful that it would make any difference. It was a problem, because people wanted to buy 24/7. Most nights before she fell asleep she would send me and whoever was around with money for cigarettes, scratch tickets, grape red vines, fun dip, sour patch explodes, donuts and apple fritters, which were her favorite. She filled the grape licorice with the sugar from the fun dip and handed them out like the loaded syringes she handed out earlier in the day. Then she would pass out and wake up in the morning raging and throwing things.

    She gave me five balloons of heroin one morning and sent me to sell them downtown, but before I took off with my bag and a long board Dreezy pulled out a huge bottle of random pills, from which I took three. I had not slept or eaten in days, and she sent me off 10 minutes later with a sweaty peck on the cheek and aggravated by how mcuh I was slurring my words.

At a store on Morrison I packed bottles of cologne into my black book bag and some fabric grocery bags I had, even though I could see stout men with earpieces watching me through the glass doors. It was the fourth time I had been there to rob the place of cologne in two weeks, and it was obvious that the men were part of a sting operation set up to stop me. I kept going anyway and juggled the five heroin balloons in my mouth with my tongue on the way out. As soon as the door opened, a voice screamed,

"STOP RIGHT THERE!!!!"

I bolted down the street after a woman working for the store scratched my neck, and I punched her. She chased me and screamed for someone to stop me. A man with long hair grabbed my backpack, and three yellow balloons fell out of my mouth and onto the sidewalk. I broke free and skated to some festival at the park by the river. There were cops looking for me, so I took off my hat and jacket, hid the skateboard under a bridge and walked around talking to strangers. Cop cars drove by every 30 seconds looking for someone but never stopped me.

Later I did the two balloons I had in my mouth, and after a few hours I went to see if the other balloons were still on the ground. They were, and I sold one and did the rest of them under a bridge as night fell, because I wasn't going back to the hotel on Mcloughlin. I told Dreezy that I messed it all up when she called, and she cried,

"Come back. I don't care. It doesn't matter to me. I want you back here. You are too important to me."

The days at Dreezy's went by hot and slow. It was June, and it seemed like everyone was in and out all day every day. We never had time together, and I could tell she wanted to get me alone. The place finally cleared out one afternoon, and I said,

"I'm leaving, too" -- to scavenge for something to trade her for more drugs.

"Why would you leave now? Huh? Everyone finally left us alone and now you want to leave? What's wrong with you?" Desperation and hurt squeezed through her voice box from across the room.

"Oh. I didn't know you wanted me to stay." I knew she wanted to have sex with me, and I felt the same, mostly from the drugs and the weird biochemical things that happen when a boy and girl spend too much time together. "I'm here, then." She put her legs up on the table, and we both grimaced at a bad smell in the room.

"I'm going to take a shower," she said.

She told everyone about it. Her friend, Gay Kevin, said that she said it was the best she had in a long time, and I was proud of myself. But as the days continued the meth overrode the heroin, and I never slept except the time she made me and I spilled water all over her in the bed. She laughed about it and changed the sheets, but she could be extremely mean too, like when I repeated myself.

"Yeah, I know, Riley. You already said that. Try saying something different. I'm tired of hearing the same old sh*t from you all the time." When I needed a haircut, she sat me down in the kitchen and cut it. She did a good job, too. I kept shaved for her because that's what she liked.

"Thanks for the hit, baby."

"Riley?"

"Yeah, baby?"

"Don't call me baby. That's not my f*cking name, and I'm not your baby!" I pretended I never heard it and referred to her as babes within a half-hour.

I stalked up and down Mcloughlin in the June sun, Quasimodo's skeleton sweating and scheming all day back and forth to the department store. Someone told me shooting up in the thin veins in my wrists was the most likely way to kill me with a clot. I didn't know if it was true, but I shot up there just in case.

Everyone told me the same thing, "You don't need a gun, Riley. Armed robbery is not worth it." But it was more about putting a bullet in the ceiling, jumping onto the counter and screaming for everyone to get on the ground. It was my new obsession but no one would give me a gun. I had fantasies of armed robbery and sweated in Dreezy's kitchen listening for cars through the blinds.

She punched me in the face one night for trying to defend myself against some grievance one of her ex-girlfriends had against me. It was getting more and more difficult to be there, and it seemed like she hated me. One night she had sex with several guys right in front of me and wouldn't look at me when I talked to her afterward. I kept trying to get her attention, but Gay Kevin said,

"Let it alone. She don't want to talk to you right now." He knew her better than I did, but I tried to grab her bags of meth and heroin to insult her. She hid the dope under her butt and told me to leave. As I made my way toward the door, one of the guys she slept with screamed obscenities and threats of stabbing me from the bathroom.

I've always heard that Teddy Roosevelt said, "Speak softly and carry a big stick." I ran my mouth and when that didn't work I used whatever I could to impose my will and destroy things. In this case it happened to be the wooden bat she kept by the door. I jumped over the bed and almost kicked the pocket door down before I pulled the guy out by his hair and drove the bat like a splitting maul to his head. It connected on the side of his skull behind his ear. He crumpled to the ground.

Dreezy jumped onto my back, so I reached behind her head and hooked her armpit to body slam her onto the floor. She gasped as the wind was knocked out of her. Gay Kevin charged me but bounced off me and went to the ground like an empty Styrofoam cup in the wind, and we spent the next few minutes in a tornado of random objects flying around the room. I launched Dreezy backwards through the air with my legs. The blinds came down with her, and she moaned like she might be seriously hurt. The men shook in fear as I backed toward the door and grabbed a sleeping bag on my way out. My stay there was up, and the cops were coming.

In a room of what were supposed to be hardened criminals, violent types, people to be feared, I was the only one living up to my persona and the things I said. Everyone bluffed and lied about the danger they presented, but like a poker game I laid down four aces almost every time the chips were on the table. They all had nothing in their hands, and you can't win with nothing when your bluff is called. It wasn't that I was tough or bad. If anything, I was a coward and selfish and stupid most of all, but I had soaked up everything I ever saw or heard like a sponge since I was little. I adapted and thrived in any environment that didn't kill me. My environments were criminal and my life was violent, so that's what I was good at.

The sirens wailed in the distance. There was a boarded-up strip club a block away where I hid in the bushes with my sleeping bag. I went back into Portland the next morning and never saw Dreezy again.

Portland-Coeur d'Alene, Idaho
Summer 2012

I wandered the streets and sniffled. I ate out of trashcans. I waited to come up and get well for the day. Sunday mornings always moved the slowest, because everyone went to church or slept in after working all week. When I called home desperate for money, "Sunday Morning" or "Face the Nation" always played on the TV tuned to CBS in the background. It was warm in my parents' bedroom on the other side of the payphone receiver, but no matter how tightly I squeezed my eyes and imagined myself back home smelling biscuits and bacon or holding a cup of black coffee, my feet never disappeared with my heart and mind over the line. They were two cold, wet bricks anchoring me to the misery of life on the streets some 2,000 miles away, hungry and sick.

It seemed like there was always a spot on my body where things had gotten hairy in the middle of an injection and I missed the vein. Sometimes the spots got infected, but they always hurt. My friends had bandages or scabs on their necks and faces. They all had suitcases they carried everywhere they went. Crimson stains of old blood that had run down my arm while trying to find a vein behind a back-alley dumpster or in a department store bathroom covered the insides of my sweatshirt sleeves. Some of my friends had track marks that looked like the lines of a rural highway system on a road map, deep purple and running up their arms toward their desperate hearts. Others of us had hematomic blobs of cloudy purple dissipating into curly tentacles of green or violet under the surfaces of our skin on our necks or arms or legs.

Deliverance from our woes came in small, brightly colored balloons, brought to us by Mexicans or Russians we called every 10 minutes hoping they might hurry. Hotel bellhops or valets stood at kiosks and glared or whispered to each other about us sitting on cold dusty pavement. We sat next to the shadows of last night's regurgitated alcohol, depraved and dying, praying for a $20 piece of salvation.

At lunch time, I could be found brazenly asking people dining at pizzerias for a slice, and if they pretended not to hear, I asked louder like they didn't speak English. When I lay behind my dumpster, it would be hard to sleep, and I would get up and walk for hours to the good ashtrays in town as if some bit of hope might be found at the bottom. I knew where the ashtrays were, like I knew where the payphones were, and can't imagine I ever walked less than 10 miles in a day.

Dealers and junkies on the street all knew me as a guy who got things for people. It was gratifying to be sought after and known for being a criminal. People asked me to get them certain clothes or electronic gear in exchange for heroin, and I obliged. If there was nothing specific to get for a dealer, then I might sell as much as $2,000 worth of stolen merchandise for a $20 bill from the African cabbies outside of the bus station.

I pretended to be normal when I went into grocery stores to steal food, like I had a car and a dog and a girlfriend and another pair of shoes in an apartment close by, and I would get into character using what I imagined was Method acting. The greatest way to project that I wasn't homeless was to believe it as reality and become one of the customers coming in to get the missing ingredients for tonight's dinner. My girlfriend was back at the apartment with my dog. The smells of yeast and flour in the bakery or bananas and watermelon in the fruit aisles helped me get into character despite my dingy clothes. Those smells provided one of the only forms of stasis in a life where everything else changed and failed.

 A ring of thieves recruited me, and we rode busses around town to hit pharmacies for their allergy medicines and vitamins or Nicorette before we rode out to meet the fence. The management at different pharmacies knew me and one other kid by name and referred to us as prolific shoplifters, which made us proud. It was always a good night for us to walk away from our efforts with five balloons apiece and each other's company, to feel like we belonged to something. One night I hit the Fred Meyers off the yellow line by myself and got chased through the parking lot before I threatened to stab the men chasing me with my dirty syringe.

 It got easier to navigate but rougher in other ways as I burnt bridges or became too well-known for stealing at certain stores, and fall would be there soon enough. It was already late June, so I made plans in over a dozen phone calls to with my mother to go to some Christian rehab in Idaho. My cousin would graduate from the rehab the weekend I arrived, and my uncle would help me get situated until I got into the program. My mother sent me $20 a day in exchange for my promised cooperation, but things were tough. All the bike cops downtown wanted to arrest me and knew me by name. Well, almost knew me by name.

"Mr. Champion, is that you?" It's actually Chapman, but I knew what the bike officer meant.

"Yes, sir." My friend Johnny Johnson and I had a $20 piece of black halfway cooked up in the bottom of an old malt liquor can, and he was showing me how to use one of the big needles to hit the vein next to my femoral artery. We sat in the bushes beside a bridge.

"Okay. Why don't you put that beer down and come see me with your friend?" The cop gave us tickets for drinking in public. Once he left, we recovered the hit in the bottom of the can and did it.

On the 4th of July, I went to watch the fireworks on the Willamette River with a stolen and unopened package of pink high-heel insoles in my pocket. Their product number matched the number on a receipt I previously found in a trashcan by

Pioneer Square. After the fireworks I went to get the cash back for the insoles. For some reason the manager wanted my ID and wouldn't do the exchange for me. We screamed at each other and threw our hands in the air before I left. It was one of my last nights in Portland.

I had promised my mother that I would cooperate and get on the bus to Idaho when the time came, but I tried to make them send me more money at the last minute and threatened to not get on the bus.

"Listen to me, Riley!" My mother spoke in a tone I had not heard much over the years. "If you don't get on that bus you can forget about calling me for anything. Ever. I'm done with you if you don't get on that bus! So, do you what you want to! It doesn't matter to me!" She hung up.

It was a Friday morning. I had previously threatened my father with becoming a freak who only talked about Jesus to make him doubt the decision to send me there. He didn't care for religion (and I wanted to keep smoking cigarettes, which would not be allowed). It wasn't true though. I would never believe in Jesus Christ. As far as I was concerned the whole story was fake. He was a fraud, and I hated him anyway.

For some reason, I got on the bus that morning and felt sad about leaving my place among the thieves and homeless addicts. Rolling out of town the streets begged me to stay. Where was I going? What did Idaho have for me? My family lived in the streets. Even if we ripped each other off and didn't have genes or parents in common we had our suffering to unify us, but now I was leaving.

I knew cross-country bus rides well, and even though this one would only be seven hours, the familiar nostalgia of passing people's entire lives and their heartaches and their joys and their childhoods and the farms where their daddy's daddy grew up eight decades before flew by in a few seconds like it was nothing, like it didn't matter. So, the scenery changed in the windows like the shapes of a kaleidoscope or the two-dimensional props of a play being flipped up, flopped down and rolled away by some invisible crew all the way to Idaho, where people ate potatoes I guessed. The two guys seated together in front of me had been released from some mental/behavioral health facility somewhere in California and were on their way home. One of them kept craning his neck and muttering about onions and potatoes. He asked the pretty girl across the aisle if she had a boyfriend. She said yes, and he asked

"How long have you had that problem?"

My uncle picked me up with my aunt and took me to eat before buying me some clothes at the Goodwill and dropping me off at the Motel 6 in Coeur d'Alene, Idaho with a fresh pack of cigarettes. It was weird to see my graduating cousin at church on Sunday praying at the altar with the other men in the program, and he prayed on stage before he gave his testimony. He gave glory to Jesus and talked about having a God-shaped hole in his heart that only God could fill. I knew then that he was brainwashed.

The next guy spoke in low-toned uncertainty to the congregation about living in his car through winter and drinking bottles of mouthwash. When the last guy picked up the microphone he enthusiastically howled in joy. The audience clapped and laughed and cheered him on. His story was one of hopelessness and a broken family. Both of his parents were addicted, and besides occasionally staying with his loving grandmother, he lived in detention centers or on the streets. He told about how the police raided his friends' tree house as kids and that once he was old enough to go to prison, he went. Whenever he got out, he went back. He said the love and family provided by the prison gangs and stability of the institutions were things he was comfortable with.

Some of his old friends went through the program years before and were successful. They paid for him to go through the ranch, and when his judge let him out of jail, the opportunity terrified him. On stage, he said he had wanted to "beat on the door of the jail" until they let him back in. He talked for 20 minutes, and people in the audience wept openly over what he said. Many of them had known him since he was a troubled teenager.

The pastor preached on the last chapter of 2 Timothy, where Paul asks his young successor to bring his coat and writings to him in a Roman prison, but I didn't care. I went outside every few minutes to smoke another cigarette. The name of the church was The Altar. There was another service on Monday night. Members of the congregation talked about God and what he was doing in their life.

One girl with curly red hair stood up and leaned her belly over the chairs in front of her to give a testimony with her powerful voice. She said she drove taxis at night and directed invisible traffic with her hands as she spoke of God's glory through her witness to fares. After an hour or so of testimony, worship began. I went out to smoke and shook my head, staring at a puddle in the street.

I officially entered the program at a Bible study at the pastor's house on Wednesday night. It was about why King James was the best version of the bible according to the pastor. The guys in the program introduced themselves to me in the van on the way back after the study. Some of them were excited to know me after they spent so much time with my cousin and teased me for it. When we got to the house the facilitator had me sign some paperwork and read the rules to me and searched my stuff. He gave me the top bunk by the window, number seven. I climbed into it as the lights went out and realized how good I felt all things considered. My thoughts blurred into sleep soon after that.

A succession of sustained piano chords on the TV speakers broke the crystal of the early-morning stillness and my slumber. The chords conveyed power, and I actually felt warm and excited about the ranch. A man's voice sang, "There is power in the name of Jesus." I knew immediately that this was special and unlike anything I had ever done in my life or would ever do again. The hope and warmth excited me in a way I didn't expect or believe was possible. It's hard to explain how or why I felt that way. I just did. It was just something about the place.

We ate breakfast. Cleaned up and sat around the living room. Cups of coffee rested between our legs. We had open Bibles in our laps. Our study of Proverbs began, and the facilitator explained how we studied the chapter that corresponded to that day of the month. It was odd for me to realize how much I didn't know about the Bible or the things inside of it. Here the book explained undeniable truth to anyone with his wits about him. Stay out of debt. Don't lie. Work hard, so you can eat. Rich people have more friends than poor people. Be kind. Don't boast about yourself or say foolish things. Let others exalt you. Proverbs offered nothing out of the ordinary.

The day continued much like any rehab does. Outside chores. Inside chores. Cook, eat and clean up lunch. We had a class called Bible tape, where we listened to the Bible and read along for 30 minutes and spent the next 30 minutes writing explanations of the verses we highlighted. Once a day, we had different teachers come in. One taught on James' epistle. Another taught relapse prevention from a biblical point of view. Twice a week we had classes at church. We had Monday night service, Bible study at the Pastor's house on Wednesday night and Sunday morning church. On Friday afternoons we split and stacked firewood for the elderly.

The pastor played piano and sang with his wife passionately and powerfully, leading worship on Sunday mornings and during Monday night services. Since I was there and had nothing to lose by doing it, I got on my face at the altar and prayed on a Monday night. I pressed my sweaty palms together and asked Jesus to reveal himself to me if he was real. He would never do it, because I knew he wasn't real.

Wednesday night of that first week, we sat under the stairs at the pastor's house. He taught us about Genesis chapter five. There appeared to be a message hidden in the fifth chapter of Genesis about the Gospel, which the Jews who wrote the first books of the Bible wouldn't have put in there and couldn't have known.

It didn't make sense. I knew that much. The Bible was a grossly inaccurate and manmade document. My confidence in that fact was a bicycle I rode at full speed, but now a piece of rebar had been put into the spokes of my front tire, launching me end over end and onto my face. The glaring inconsistency between what I thought I knew and what was actually in the Bible left me reeling.

Not a whole lot changed for me after that, because I didn't believe whatever they thought I was supposed to and any time evolution was brought up, I balked and undermined the teachers. Out of the facilitator's earshot I made plans to run the potent white powder heroin of Dayton, Ohio, across the country to Taos. I would capitalize on my newfound sobriety and the isolated market in Taos. In one of my classes I told the teacher that I was meant for more than not doing drugs and not living that old life. During Proverbs studies in the morning, I managed to get three of the men to go silent and glare at me, because my words and ways were so incendiary.

After 60 days I graduated on stage like everyone does. My parents and my uncle came up to visit and stood with me. They shed tears over the emotional nature of it all, and when I got up to the microphone I said something I didn't believe about God plucking me out of the fire and saving me. The pastor whispered in agreement. My right arm jerked from involuntary spasms of nervousness.

We all prayed on stage before we sat down for the rest of the two-hour service. One of my friends from the ranch had dreadlocks and graduated two weeks before me. He took me to the store. I tried to smoke old, wet cigarette butts out of the ashtray. Smoking was against the rules and a sure way to get kicked out of the halfway house run by one of the guys from the program. It was the only place I had to live, and they kicked me out in the middle of October for smoking, besides the relationship I had with a single mother in the congregation.

They kicked me out Friday night. Saturday afternoon I smoked weed, and on Sunday morning I injected half of a Subutex my friend with the dreadlocks had gotten me on top of Tubbs Hill by the lake. It wasn't fun, and I puked my guts up at the Dairy Queen while my friends ate ice cream. My friend with dreadlocks let me use his Sub Zero sleeping bag to sleep in a shipping container behind Safeway. Going to service at church got me out of the cold. Greasy black rings formed on my collar and sleeve cuffs. I had dime- sized pupils and held my jaw in that funny way that only people on meth do. Sometimes I would nod out and wake up with a loud hiccup in the quiet between worship songs or during a sermon. Everyone would stare at me.

The girl with curly red hair gave me a Christian CD to help me avoid music about drugs. She prayed for me on more than one occasion and was a charismatic leader in our church. Her words and actions testified of God's real power to save a hopelessly addicted and miserable person like her, even someone like me. We called her Faith, and I always joked that if she answered her phone then the Rapture hadn't happened.

Homelessness continued until I got a job and had my first day of work. On December 17, my uncle came to town to help move my cousin out of one apartment and into another. He would help me find one to move into, too. I would pay rent with the money from my new job at the burger joint in the Safeway parking lot.

My uncle put me and my cousin in a hotel room while he was in town. Our first night at La Quinta Inn at the end of Sherman, Faith and I chatted on Facebook and eventually talked on the phone. I did a weak shot of heroin before she called.

"Well, what do you think is causing you to feel separated from the Lord, Riley?"

"I don't know. It's not drugs. I smoke cigarettes, but I don't think that's it."

"Yeah! I definitely think a person can smoke and be in true relationship with the Lord, but do you realize that Jesus wants to set you free of that bondage? He has so much more for you. He has so much more for us. The Word says exceedingly abundantly above anything that we could ever think or ask! Ha ha! I love Ephesians!"

"Yeah. Ephesians is cool, but I haven't read it lately. It's very hard for me to believe that the Word is the truth. I was raised with evolution and went to school to be a veterinarian, so I was a biology major. Evolutionary science has been reality my whole life, and I can't seem to get around it. The Bible seems like a storybook to me."

"Hmmmm... So, you think your faith is wavering? James 1:8: A double minded man is unstable in all his ways! Don't be double minded! Haha!"

"Wavering? If it was wavering I'd be doing great. I don't know." I drew smoke from my cigarette and into my lungs.

"I see. Maybe we can get together tomorrow to pray about it. Are you free tomorrow?"

"Yeah. I think so. 10:30 at Java would work for me. I have to go with my uncle to find a place to rent in town."

"Okay. I'll be praying for you tonight. Tomorrow, we'll get together for some prayer. Will you pray for my brother?"

"Sure. Younger or older?"

"My little brother. He's been doing meth and hard drugs. He's on felony probation, but he needs to get saved."

"Sure. I'll pray for him."

"Thanks."

"Hey, Faith. I love you. You know? Not like that, but I do. You are very cool, and I am thankful for you."

"Ha ha. Yeah. I know. I love you, too. That's what we're supposed to do. I appreciate that."

"Okay. Good night, Faith."

"'Night, Riley."

The next morning, my uncle and aunt dropped me off at the coffee shop on the corner of Fourth and Sherman. It was a place for hipsters and pot smokers, but some people had Bibles out while they drank their coffee. Faith wore a baby-blue knit cap to cover her uncombed red hair, and the drab shirt she wore hung loose from her poorly postured shoulders. She ordered what appeared to be sugar and milk on ice in a plastic cup with a straw and sat down across from me with her Bible, a notebook and a pen. For whatever lack of effort she appeared to put into her appearance, she was pretty. Her teeth were straight, and her green eyes radiated a glowing joy that made me uncomfortable about the gloom hiding behind my own.

"I want you to read Romans chapter one."

"Okay."

"Where's your Bible?"

"I don't have it."

"Okay. Use mine." I moved my eyes from word to word. Romans seemed impossible to understand. Much of the Bible seemed to be that way for me, except for the history.

"Read it out loud," she said, so I did.

After the first chapter she asked me to read three more, and after the fourth chapter we talked for a while. She asked me what I struggled with, and I mentioned cigarettes, doubt, anger, using harsh words, an identity bound up in hopelessness, homelessness and resentment, everything but the heroin and pornography. Faith asked me about family curses passed down to me. I shook my head like I didn't know. The whole notion sounded ridiculous to me. Either I learned violence and intimidation from my father or I didn't. Either, my grandfather was an alcoholic and I was predisposed to addiction because of that or I wasn't. My brainwaves could either be tested with scientific instruments showing me to be bipolar or not. There was no such thing as a curse in my eyes.

For half an hour, we prayed with our hands clasped over the table. She went through the list of things she had written down. It was nothing eloquent, only that these issues were being submitted to the Lord and that his will would be done. His will was that sin and curses would be broken off my life, and I wanted that. I didn't believe it could happen, because I didn't believe in God.

My uncle and aunt sat at a table and allowed the prayer to continue. When I looked up to see them I felt slightly ashamed for Faith's appearance as if my own were any better. It would have looked like she and I were romantically involved, and it embarrassed me. It was time to go look for a place with them.

"Faith, I really appreciate you. Thank you so much for coming to pray for me and see me. I don't know if it worked, but something has to work sometime."

"Yeah! Ha ha! Don't stop praying. Here's the list. Pray this over yourself as much as possible. Prayer is like working out. You can't go to the gym once and expect major results. Keep praying. I will be."

"Thank you. I have to go now."

My aunt and uncle took me to look at a couple of places before we found a place close to downtown on Foster Avenue. Once they left I moved into my cousins and slept on his couch so I could watch Netflix and use the Wi-Fi. My friend from the program rented the place my uncle had gotten me on Foster with another friend of his. They paid me 250$ each for a total of $500 a month, but when it was time to pay the rent, I had already used the money they gave me to get high. My mother sent me another $500 to pay the rent. I spent that on heroin and meth, too. Finally, my mother took over paying rent at the place on Foster to avoid screwing my uncle over, who had put his name on the lease.

While I lived at my cousins, I did copious amounts of heroin and meth behind the scenes. My manager at work caught me with a syringe behind my ear. Another guy I had been through the program with came to my cousin's place to pray for me, but I threatened to stab myself and screamed at him in my boxers. A week after that I had calmed down and that same guy came to take me to a Monday night service. It had been a few months since I had been to a service. Faith was there. The pastor preached a sermon on casting off darkness to put on light and used me as an example for what happens when you do too many drugs and forsake God's mercy. I was sweating and flailing in the front row of church.

My legs always hurt at work. It was a symptom of daily heroin withdrawals. I talked back to management and could barely do the work they had for me and maintained a sloppy appearance. One time, they caught me stealing a cigarette out of another kid's pack and another time, I snuck around the back and stole the $3 out of the tip jar on the drive-through window.

My cousin continued to let me stay with him, until I took some Xanax one night and set his porch on fire. It was no fun moving back to the apartment on Foster without Netflix or Wi-Fi. Desperation sank into my mind and emotions. I walked miles up to work and miles back at night. Maintaining my heroin habit became nearly impossible with the meager wages and lack of hours at the burger joint.

I stayed awake on meth for three days and nights once and called my parents from the apartment. There was no reason that I can remember calling. But that phone call would be the catalyst to change my life.

My father's father died of pneumonia when I was 11 years old. His mind deteriorated from Alzheimer's first, and then he couldn't walk. Too much time in bed led to bed sores and after something like seven years of not knowing where he was, pneumonia developed. My sisters and I knew my father had aged and seemed different from the way he had been our whole lives. He never gave us a straight answer, and my mom denied anything was happening.

"Mama, what's wrong with Poppa?"

"Hmmmmm... What do you mean?"

"You know what I mean. He's different. Does he have Alzheimer's?" The background noise of words and voices on the TV came over the line during her silence. She thought for a moment more, before she responded,

"I'll let you ask him yourself. Let me get him." A few moments later I heard her say, "Kelly. It's Riley. He wants to ask you something."

"Riley? How are you?" The kindness in his voice proved to me that something was different with him. For years both of them always sounded so disappointed with me, and there was no reason why they wouldn't be now. He spoke softer and sweeter, like he didn't remember the trouble I always caused them or maybe didn't care anymore. My insides braced for what I was about to hear.

"Good." I choked.

"What's up?"

"Poppa, what's wrong with you?" There was no easy way to ask the question.

He laughed like he always did when things got serious or emotional. "How can you tell something's wrong?"

"I just can. You're not the same. What is it?"

"I have Parkinson's." The words broke me in half. For more than a decade I tried to kill him by killing myself, but now that I finally had everything I thought I ever wanted, I didn't want it anymore. He couldn't hear me cry because the wind was knocked out of me, and I didn't know what to do.

My friend gave me the name of a doctor who wrote prescriptions for Xanax, but when I visited him, he would only write a prescription for Paxil, an SSRI antidepressant. Paxil has no recreational side effects, so I never took it. The anxiety continued, even though I went back to church and read the Bible when I woke up every night from nightmares of my life being violently ripped from me.

I threw my ranch Bible off my bed and onto the floor one night after I found out about my dad. The Bible was too much for me to believe even if I wanted to. Creation. A flood. Parting the Red Sea. Fire and brimstone. The dead coming back to life and all the rest of it. "If God wanted me to believe the Bible," I thought, "then, why did he make it a f*cking storybook?" Those were the exact words in my head as I pushed the ember of my cigarette butt straight down into the ashtray and twisted. I pulled the chain on my reading lamp and fell back onto the bed, pulling the covers over my shoulder. Christ wasn't real, and he sure couldn't save me.

I woke up a few hours later with the same nightmare of being murdered. The Bible was too much to believe, but my desperation overrode my disillusioned disposition long enough for me to pick it up off the floor. I turned to Psalms to comfort me in place of the chemicals my brain and body were accustomed to, because the Psalms were short, easy passages. I read Psalm 120. Verse six says, *My soul hath long dwelt with him that hateth peace,* and I thought to myself that it sounded appropriate for my life of running with the devil and hurting everyone.

I moved onto the next Psalm, and as I read the first verse, it was instantly clear to me that my life had been supernaturally saved by an almighty and all-wise God. As surely as I breathe and write this, more certainly than my name is Riley Chapman, I know I received eternal life and salvation. The miracle that took place inside of me dwarfed the supernatural acts I so doubted in the Bible. Creation itself could not compare to the glory at work inside of my chest and head. God wrote those scriptures for me and to save me before time ever was and waited an eternity for me to find them. He called my name, and that was it. It was finished.

I worry that telling you about my life in Christ will alienate you the reader from me the writer. That would be terrible. This is something I share with the sincerest of sincerity about my life and where it has ended up. If you don't believe, I understand. It was impossible for me to believe until the miracle happened. I love you anyway and more so because of it. Let me share with you some of the things Christians believe. Maybe it will help you understand how difficult it was for me to come to faith.

They believe that an invisible and almighty and eternal God created everything out of nothing. He made the first man out of mud and breathed into it to give him life. God made the first woman out of the first man's rib. There was a flood over the face of the planet that killed all but eight people. God's people, the Israelites, were enslaved for 400 years before he delivered them by parting the Red Sea and led them in the desert by a pillar of smoke in the day and fire by night. His prophets raised the dead and called down fire from heaven. After centuries of the Israelites' disobedience toward him, God sends his own son, who is also God, to live as a transient, poor carpenter/teacher and die bloody on a cross for the sins of all mankind. Christians believe in an eternal life in the presence of God and eternal hell outside of his presence and that the only way to live forever is to forsake your life and live for Christ. There's more to it than all of that. But that gives you an idea of some of it.

Now, the only thing crazier than everything I just told you about Christianity was myself the day after I got saved. There were certain things about the gospel I could identify with. Jesus said the world hated him and the world would hate us for following him. I knew how to be hated. He called his followers to die. My own death fascinated me for years. Now I could do it for the right reasons.

It wasn't as if I forgot suddenly the injustices committed in the name of the Lord or the grievances the world held against Christianity and Christ himself. The Catholic church, I felt, had done terrible things. Martin Luther led the protestant Reformation to save Christianity from the Vatican, but he also wrote large amounts of anti-Semitic literature. Racist organizations such as the KKK or Aryan Nation claim to follow Christ and read the Bible. What I had to realize was that Christ said nothing these men did. They were men mishandling the gospel of grace so powerfully and lovingly shared by my Savior in the first century. For me being Christian was the ultimate counter-culture -- truly being Christian, not as a matter of identity or favor in the eyes of men, but as a servant humbly loving those who hate him and dying for an invisible kingdom not made with hands. Hatred, fear, ignorance, war and force are the greatest expressions of failure as a Christian.

My apartment on Foster continued to stink, and different dealers or alcoholics or junkies stopped by every day to see me or my roommate. I smoked as many cigarettes as I could and all my clothes smelled like the fryer grease at the burger joint, until I quit because of the drugs people did at work. Anyone who offered me drugs at my house had to go. I was kind but unwavering on the prohibition of pills or meth at my house.

I hung out with Faith every day after that. She inspired me to live a life of holiness by her own steadfast devotion to God and the Word. She showed me what life in him could look like, and that it was cool and fun. We lived a few blocks away from each other and spent our days listening to music or at the park with her dog.

Everyone always said that we were a good fit for each other, but attraction did not exist between us. She was my friend, and I was hers. We spent all our time together. We worked out together. We ate together. I washed dishes at the Greek restaurant where she served tables, and our Greek boss commented that I would make a baby come out of her one day.

It wasn't what I wanted, but I prayed to God that if it was his will then he would have to turn my heart toward her.

I tried to quit smoking eight times before I succeeded while Faith started smoking for the first time in three years. There were roommates coming and going at the apartment doing drugs or drinking against my wishes and my mom still paid the rent for some reason. She could tell something had changed in me and felt happy to help since I was doing so well. Faith loved working at the ranch and ministering to the women there, but she lost her job over the cigarettes that she started smoking with me.

July of 2013 was the first month of my life without cigarettes, marijuana or any drugs. It was hard to believe that my life changed like that, and that it was so easy. The chains of drug addiction and violence had me bound for over a decade by then, and on my birthday a leader in the church publicly exhorted me at our Friday night potluck for the obvious change in my life. I wept for God's grace on my life at 27 years old.

There was still a lot to be worked through though. I continued to look at pornography on a laptop that I had and confessed my sin and powerlessness to Christian brothers regularly. Aside from being completely unholy in my private life concerning the images at which I looked, I was self-righteous and very vocal about it. Something about the pornography provoked bouts of self-righteous snobbery, which I used to beat other people down about doing yoga or drugs. It was the sin commonly known as hypocrisy in the church and the most common charge against it by the unbelieving world. My inability to abstain from pornography could be forgiven with confession and prayer according to the Bible, and I did those things. But the hypocrisy came when I judged others for their sins, which may have been more obvious but not worse than mine. I was as powerless as anyone else.

In August I moved out of the apartment on Foster and into a discipleship house several blocks away. It was fall by then, and they found the dead body of one of Faith's best friends. He had graduated from the ranch, and Faith knew him for years before and after she came to Christ, so her testimony was paramount in his decision to go through the program. The untimely and self-inflicted death of a close friend hurts, especially if you were supposed to be with him the moment he did his last injection and died cold and alone by the river.

Faith forgot to call him when she went to Monday night service. They were supposed to go together, and besides that she blamed herself for smoking cigarettes and not being the shining testimony he expected her to be when he got out of the ranch.

Unexpected emotion came over me at our friend's house as Faith wept and slept wrapped in a blanket next to me on the couch. There was an overwhelming desire to take care of her, to protect her, and I felt like I loved her as something more than a friend for the first time. I wanted to wipe away her tears. I wanted to hold her.

I confessed it to her over lunch at a Mexican restaurant with our friend. She wouldn't look up from her plate and shook her head after she told me to stop. It was right after she told us that she was moving to Spokane for beauty school to deal with our friend's death. I knew she would fight me, but I knew she needed me even though she never admitted it and said she didn't want me. No one knew her like me. No one loved her like me.

My parents paid for me to fly home seven months after I got saved. It was at Christmas time, and my mother's whole family went to eat at Clancy's. Our grandmother and her boyfriend sat at the head of the big table by me, and I pretended to understand what the deaf old man was talking about. Right before the main course was served up, I turned my chair away from them. I hadn't thought much of it for the last eight years, but I had been gone and lost and dead in so many ways. Here I was after all of it like I never left, and no one seemed to notice the significance of it. I turned my chair and wept like a man wrongly imprisoned and finally returned to his family. It wasn't wrongful, but it was a prison inside of myself like that. Now I was free, and all I could do was weep for the mercy and grace upon my life.

  Carlos happened to be in town, so Timothy and Jerry, the guys who had started making the documentary about me years before, came by to get an interview from me after several years of us hearing nothing from them. In the interview, I breathed hard at 260 pounds and rubbed my palms with nervous energy while I listened to their questions. I testified boldly of God's grace and power to save my life through his word. I smoked no cigarettes in the two hours we talked and used silliness instead of the s word and baloney instead of b.s. Toward the end Carlos wished me good luck, but I turned him down for it. He laughed when I said I didn't need it because God is in control.

The power of what God had done in my life was hard for them to deny, however skeptical they were. There was no question that something dramatic had taken place in my life, but the answer I gave them was not what they wanted. At a coffee shop Jerry and Timothy asked me about the morality of the Bible. Masturbation and pornography came up, and I could not testify of much victory in my life concerning those things. They remained unconvinced.

My mother recalled my years on the street and what it was like for her. She said,

"I could go out and dance to the hottest live music in town. I could drink the finest wine and laugh all night, but when I came home and wiped the makeup off my face and turned the lights out, there was only you." The statement hit me hard. My father and I didn't fight the whole week I was there. It was an amazing visit and A milestone for my parents to have such peace and obvious change in their son.

Before I left on Christmas day, my mother gave me a pair of silver cross earrings she had bought in Mexico. I specifically asked for them to give to Faith, and when I got back to town, Faith and I watched Christmas movies on the couch at her mom's house. It was nice to be back, and I wanted her mom to be my mother-in- law. Her mom wanted me to be her son-in-law. Faith sent me a picture of herself wearing the earrings to say thank you, but after that, things continued as they had before, awkward and one-sided.

Idaho

2014-2016

Sometimes I felt like Nero watching his beloved Rome burn to the ground while he played the violin. I loved to set things on fire, and I loved to watch them burn. But in the decade of my self-inflicted holocaust, the only music I ever heard was my own weeping and teeth gnashing.

Now, I look at my hands and wonder why I let them tear everything down for so long.

My friend told me that Faith had gotten drunk with her a few weeks before, and Faith had fallen in other ways too. It was a cold January afternoon when I found out, and I cursed for the first time in more than half a year. The girl meant everything to me and led me to Jesus with a vibrant passion for his presence. She forgot what she was worth and so made her appeals to men on a biochemical level, because she knew we would never see in her what she could not see in herself. Now she traded eternal glory for their attention and the emptiness of mind-altering substances. It killed me inside. Her distress and the distance between us compounded to turn my love into an unhealthy obsession.

My depression grew while I learned a certain amount of obedience through the suffering. I quit looking at porn so much, though I still fell from time to time, and my calling as a Bible teacher became clear among my peers. My room stayed a mess. I got fatter. My appearance never improved. I desperately wanted to become a man that Faith could expect to take care of her, so I prayed that God would give me a job with overtime, help me lose weight and get a car. He answered quickly with a job at a Vietnamese pho restaurant.

On a Tuesday morning my friend dropped me off at the pho. A short old man in a hat and glasses let me in before he shuffled toward a table and pulled out a chair. His open hand indicated that the seat was for me. I sat down, and he sat at an adjacent table by the window. He drank tea from a small glass and smiled. One look at the place, and I actually thought it was a money-laundering front for an Asian gangster out of Seattle.

"You like work?"

"Yes. I like work!"

"Good. Me..." He stuck his thumb into his chest. "83 already. Twenty-four year work every day, man. No drink water. Beer only. Ya! No beer! No work!"

"Ha ha. What's your name?"

"Sau." He continued to talk to me about his life and work habits in broken English. He told of his disdain for Washington state and the difficulties of running a small business there and the drug-addicted homeless population. That was why he had moved over to Idaho to sell pho about 10 years before. Then he asked, "You like Vietnamese girl?" I knew from my time in Peru what he was thinking. Citizenship.

"Yes. I like Vietnamese girl." I didn't see any reason to not like a Vietnamese girl but not in the way he meant it.

"Maybe I find girl for you. Good girl. Vietnamese girl. Marry you. Yeah. Good Vietnamese girl." He looked at me seriously, showing the only two teeth he had sticking out of his bottom gum, and I laughed at the prospect. I would not marry an unbeliever as a Christian and sought to explain to him what that meant for me and how it worked. For the first six months that I worked there, when he got drunk and saw me, he always said, "No smoke. No beer. Girl only! Ha ha ha." His laugh and face should have been put on a list of the 20 cutest things in the world.

Toward the middle of one day Sau asked me if I liked working for him and said if I wanted the job, I would have to work 16 days in a row. Between my anxiety and depression over Faith and working at the pho so much, I could feel a significant amount of weight had come off of me in just two weeks.

Sau paid me $1,100 for those 16 days, and I took Faith to her favorite breakfast spot on a Sunday morning before I went in to work. I gave her a four-page love letter written on yellow paper. She grimaced when she knew what it was and suggested that I keep it. It was about the kind of love that only exists between best friends and talked of resting my head in her lap after work, dancing with her in our living room on Friday nights, making love on Saturday morning while the eggs and toast burned, wiping her tears with my own cheeks and warming her feet between mine at night. I wanted a life with her with everything that was inside of me, but she took me to work after breakfast without saying much.

As the money continued I got a membership at the CrossFit gym where Faith worked out before she moved to Spokane for beauty school. The weight continued to come off me, and my shoulders and arms took shape. Other girls at church noticed me and texted me, but I could only think of Faith. When she flunked out of school and couldn't pay rent anymore, I rented a U-haul and moved all her stuff to a storage unit in Coeur d'Alene that I paid for. She wouldn't ride in the truck with me after all I did for her. It was a perfect opportunity to see her selfishness and lack of interest in me, but I couldn't. I was blinded by love.

Within three months I bought a beautiful black 1994 Lexus ES 300 from one of Sau's sons. He gave me a great deal, and now I had the car, the money, the attention from girls, the productivity of being sober and what I assumed was a tip on big-time Asian heroin dealers through one of Sau's kids who worked with me. Even if they didn't mess around they had a cousin in California or Philadelphia who could help me out, and I had money, a car and a head clear enough to make all of my fantasies of smuggling and dealing China white heroin across the country come true. Faith had already started using illicit drugs, and it would be a sure way to get her attention.

It never happened though, because Faith got a boyfriend and I got a job at the ranch as a nighttime facilitator. My faith and life in Christ grew tremendously as I pastored a group of men who lived with me in the truth and who called me out. It was an amazing time, but at night when the lights went out at night I cried on my bedroom floor until snot hung from my lip and my face got splotchy. Faith had forfeited God's grace for a life of drugs, and it killed me.

Faith and I didn't talk for a long time so I got over it and smiled again, but she contacted me in early winter and let me take her to sushi. She was living in Post Falls with a guy she sold for and had a pair of binoculars with her when I picked her up that night. It was nice to be with her again, and before I took her back to the place in Post Falls she let me pray for her in my car. Tears streamed down her face as I held my palm against the top of her head and prayed. I wiped the tears from her cheeks with my thumb, and she pushed her face into my hand. Before long I held her in my arms and stroked her hair like I always wanted. It was obvious that this was what she always wanted too.

"I always had to ask myself if you were the one, Riley," she confessed. It was a hook that sank deep into my heart. I always bit for her. I loved her.

I had been seeing another girl. But it fizzled, and Faith continued to ignore my texts after that night. It was Dec. 6 when her new boyfriend and dealer got arrested. Our pastor used her boyfriend's incarceration as leverage to get Faith back in for a one month kicker back in the ranch, but there was no funding according to her mom. I called the pastor and gave my whole paycheck to the church secretary that month for Faith's ranch fund.

Other girls liked me, and I found out later that Faith said terrible things about me at the ranch. I had paid knowing full well that she only wanted to get her boyfriend into the ranch, and after two weeks of her month-long kicker, she left. It wasn't as hard to take as I would have thought, and she apologized to me for wasting my money. Her excuses made sense to her, and I didn't expect anything different. So, I let it go. We didn't talk for months after that development, and my life in the Lord continued to grow in leaps and bounds. Colors got brighter, and food tasted better. Every day seemed to be the best day of my life with her out of my mind.

It lasted the summer. She came back around in fall when her newest ex-boyfriend had to go through the ranch where I worked at night. He gave me tons of grief, and she did everything she could to make it worse by befriending me again. He saw us together at church and took it out on me at work by talking bad about me to the other men. I would forgive him and ask for forgiveness in front of the whole house three times a week. I practiced humility even if he would never drop the issue and I kept my emotional guard up from her this time.

When her ex-boyfriend relapsed and went back to jail, she went off on a runner shooting meth and selling drugs. I didn't get bent out of shape over it this time, but she came to church one Monday night and prayed with me. She broke down and asked me to come see her at her mom's in the morning, so I did. We went to Atilanos, and she ate tacos while I played Sudoku on my phone and maintained my apathy.

"Riley, I need help. I need you to be my friend." Her green eyes conveyed a sense of sincerity that I had never seen in her before.

"Yeah. Well. I don't know what to tell you, Faith."

"What do you mean?"

"I mean I'm done. There's no point in being part of your life anymore."

"Why?" Her tone was desperate.

"Because you don't care. You don't listen. You love your sin and your delusions of being a gangster and all of it! It has nothing to do with me. There's nothing I can do for you."

"Please, Riley. I love you and need you to be in my life. You are my only real friend." She had other friends but none of them knew how to love her and do what was best for her in spite of however difficult she made it.

"I don't... I don't know if I can waste my time any more. It's gotten old."

"Okay." She held back tears. "I understand."

On Jan. 1, I started a 10-day fast to ask the Lord for his intervention in her life. It was obvious that I needed to be healed of whatever kept me involved with such unhealthy behavior. She was like a bag of heroin. All the years I was addicted I convinced my chemical free self that one bag or one hit of heroin wouldn't take me to all of the miserable places it always did. This time it'll be different, I told myself. This time I won't get strung out or rob anyone or lie, but I always did. My relationship with her was as irrational, and I always came back. I needed a miracle again like I did that night in my bed when God delivered me from drug addiction.

Well, he delivered me and intervened in her life. Within 26 hours of the fast she had her first felonies and sat in jail awaiting arraignment. The deliverance for me was much messier and more painful and slower than that night in my bed when he saved me from myself and drugs. This time I cried and wavered internally for months while she was in jail. I wrote her and she wrote back. We exchanged harsh words through our correspondence. It took me almost two months to visit her, and when I did I told her that I would pay for her to get into the ranch again. She owned me, and I let her know. But that night I determined to go back in the morning and tell her it was over for good. When she saw me on the other side of the glass she looked disappointed that it was me visiting her. She preferred someone with a neck tattoo or a wife and kids but picked up the phone to talk to me anyway.

"Hey."

"So, I'm sorry for the things I said yesterday. I'm not going to pay for the ranch. In fact, I don't care what you do. I'm finished. For real. I hope things change for you and that you come to the Lord, but I'm done. I don't care if I ever see you again, Faith."

"Okay."

"You must have known this would eventually come. Is there anything you want to say?"

"Not really."

"Okay. Bye." I hung up the receiver, and she smashed hers against the window and screamed profanity at me. I walked away, but by Wednesday of that week I felt the depression and fear of not having her in my life again.

For all of the pain and suffering drugs had caused me in life, I knew what they were and how to suffer and be miserable with them. I filled myself up with the pain and hid my life in them, but since I had quit them some years before, she was the new source of pain. She was predictable, so I didn't have to fear the unknown like I would without her. My identity should have been hidden in Christ, not in anything or anyone else, and my God would be faithful and deliver his son from the chains of sin and suffering I found myself bound up in.

I had had broken hearts before and blamed myself for being so terrible to the women I knew, but none of them had ever had this kind of power over me. None of them controlled me or used me. That was my job. That's what I did, but now Faith used me. She hurt me, and I let her for years. I learned what it was like to love someone who didn't love herself and who would use me to get what she wanted; it was like everything my father and mother went through with me. God would have to perform a miracle to set me free, and he did when I asked my pastor's wife to pray for me by the Wednesday of that week.

By Friday night I got the flu for the second time in 29 years, and there seemed to be some sort of nervous breakdown behind the sickness. I locked myself in my room and drank some Nyquil before hallucinations of spiritual powers plagued me over the weekend. In my fevered dreams, it seemed as if God was removing things that looked like kidney stones out of my chest and throat and face where the depression and fear were hidden inside of me.

Traumatized by the experience, I determined to not go back to Faith no matter what I felt, and what I felt about her decreased steadily thereafter. God confirmed that our complete separation was the right thing in his Word. In the book of Ezra, the Israelites who are supposed to be rebuilding the temple got distracted for something like 20 years with heathen wives and had families and built whole lives through the ungodly unions. In response God commands them to abandon their strange wives and their children and homes to get back to God's plan for them as a people. It would have been unimaginably difficult to leave behind all that they loved, but God gave them three days to separate themselves and return to what was right. I prayed for God's voice before I read that day and knew he was speaking to me about Faith.

She did a year and then some in prison on her charges. Now she comes around and seems to be better than she has been in years. We don't talk though, not out of spite or anything like that. It's just that she doesn't have anything for me, and I don't have anything for her. Our lives have gone in different directions.

Idaho

Present

2 Peter 1:3,4

According as his divine power hath given unto us all things that pertain unto life and godliness, through the knowledge of him that hath called us to glory and virtue:

Whereby are given unto us exceeding great and precious promises that by these we might be partakers of the divine nature, having escaped the corruption that is in the world through lust.

I wouldn't want the pain and embarrassment of what I went through with Faith to overshadow my relationship with the Lord. It was sinful and wrong to exalt her in my mind and heart the way that I did. Enduring the pain of letting it go, however unfruitful and one-sided it was, and trusting God for something else has been the greatest display of faith in my life. She taught me a lot about myself.

Since then, and during the turmoil, God has worked miracles in my life. I went to get my genotype and viral load tests done so I could start some therapy for my Hepatitis. When the results came back, the doctor told me I didn't have it at all. There is a small percentage of people whose bodies fight it off naturally. I'm also HIV negative, which is equally miraculous.

God has tempered me because my zealotry for Christ put people off those first two years. There was one instance in which I back my father into a corner of the house and literally beat my Bible with my hand as I testify of its power and truth. I didn't tell him that he was going to hell or anything like that but proclaimed that the accuracy of prophecies throughout the book proved the faith to be something so much more than man's contrivance. Not everyone feels the same way, and God taught me to be patient with those who didn't believe. He showed me that the most profound testimony to his existence could not be professed. It could only be seen. For those first couple of years I was so focused on being right that I missed the fact that no one cared if I was. Now I build relationships of love and concern for others, never compromising on the gospel as it applies to me.

I am an administrator for one of the three men's houses and am a leader in our church by default more than anything else. The nature of our church is one of outreach, particularly toward the criminal and drug-addicted community. It is a hard battle to wage in the small town of Coeur d'Alene because it seems like everyone does drugs or has at one point or another. It is in the brokenness of these men that I continue to heal by pouring myself out for their sake. Loving them is what my life is about, but sometimes they minister to me by loving me. Other times they are so critical and negative, I have to be on my game so they don't have that ammunition.

Working at the ranch keeps me thankful for the freedom I have today. Middle-aged men come in with yellow eyes and black scabs on their swollen faces like I used to have. They've told lies for so long they don't know the truth or who they are. After a few days light returns to their countenance and strength to their voices. Sometimes, great breakthrough happens, and they decide to do anything necessary to be sober and follow Christ. Other times, they cause nothing but a stink until they leave. There are those who stare down from dark eyes. They pick black from under their nails and twiddle fingers, like they are sewing together the string of words squeezing out of them one at a time. I get brainiacs who sought to be "heads" on the hippy end of the dope world spectrum. Many of the younger men do pushups and focus on working out or beating me at ping pong.

The harder the client is, the more affection I show them. I see so much of myself in a man who hates Christianity and authority and even himself. My heart cries to help them. Nothing is more rewarding than hearing these men share how my example and love has softened them and shown them a different way. Twice, I have had to take my glasses off when men have confronted me. I remain peaceful and soft-spoken in spite of their yelling, but eyeglasses cost money, and there is no point in letting them get ruined on top of having a broken nose. Only love combats hatred and anger. I finally realize that.

We see great success in the men and women who graduate from the program. Often, that success comes after a few falls, but some of them make it happen the first time. There are plenty of examples of men and women who have to serve out some time, because they continue to break the law or use while on probation. Sometimes, they overdose or commit suicide, and it hurts. The cause keeps me going, though. This is God's work, and I am committed to doing it. He is not a concept or an accessory to my identity. He is someone I know. He is my all. Some mornings I weep with a heart of compassion he gives me. Evenings I laugh in joy for all he has done.

The cast of characters I call my friends is no less colorful than it was when I did drugs. One of my friends led a local Satanic sex cult and struggles to maintain any length of sobriety, as do many of my friends. He says crazy things and thinks people are always coming to kill him. Another buys cases of spoiled protein drinks from the discount grocery store and brags about paying 25 cents per bottle. He usually gives me one and is so excited to watch me drink it. I take a few sips, hiding my grimace. When he isn't looking I pour it out or carry it away and hide it. One of those soured protein drinks is sitting on my desk as I type this. I have another friend who tucks his hernia in like a shirttail and whose weight fluctuates between 300 and 500 pounds. He tells me he's convinced the devil gave him his phone so he could use the hard drive from it as evidence against him on the day of judgement. We laugh about ourselves and how broken we all are.

One of the greatest ways God changed me came through my job at the pho working for the old man. I worked at least 60 hours a week for the first six months, but when the pastor asked me to work at the ranch, I had to quit. When the plans were in place to start working there, I told the old man that I had to go as I poured two bowls of soup for him to serve before anyone else had come into work. He looked sad and said,

"I love you." Now, I don't know what he thought he was saying, but I know that the Vietnamese understand love. He never said it again. When I told him, I loved him after that, he acted like he didn't hear me.

I worked Fridays at the pho while I worked at the ranch the rest of the week, and three years after I tried to quit, I still work there. It was my idea that I would culturally enrich myself and learn Vietnamese while I worked there, but after so much time getting nothing but perplexed looks, I have opted to scream back in the same broken English they speak. "Lotta peepo?" means "Are there a lot of people?" "Vechaybo" is vegetable. And you get the point.

While I was eating lunch there about a year ago with a friend, Sau jumped up from his seat and beer by the window and ran to the back. He returned and proudly dropped a packet of papers on the table and told me to look with an excited smile. I read that they were contracts for burial plots at the cemetery in town.

"Maybe, next yee uh I sleep dare. Ya! Sleep! I tie-od, man!" I smiled at his excitement and hoped he wouldn't die any time soon. A month after that his oldest son called me into work early in the morning. I found out that the old man had missed work for the first time in 25 years. A week later he missed once more, and he never worked again. His son took over the 5 a.m. prep, and the old man had to stay in the hospital for a short stay. The last time I saw him was right before Christmas. Fidel Castro had recently died. I dropped something off at his house, and he jumped up to offer me a small bottle of orange juice. He stared at the ground and smiled before he gave me a $100 bill for a

Christmas present. His wife died a few months after him, and when I dream of him, I wake up bawling.

My mother told me on the phone that her father had died, and it was quick. The last time I saw Turkey, he was on his walker and had started smoking cigarettes, which was weird. He told me that if I got back on the drugs again, we would have to take a trip to the hospital, so I asked him why.

"So they can pull my foot out of you're a**, Riley. That's why!"

My mom's mother, Grand Mary, who always called me her No. 1 grandson and who took me to the ghetto that Sunday morning before work a decade ago, died a month or so ago. I saw her right before it happened, and we had a good time talking to each other. She showed me so much about life and always sent the funniest Bitmojis of herself over text message because her voice had quit working so well a few years back. I miss her already.

My dad's mom took all my phone calls when I ran around the streets with Danielle in Denver. I used to keep her on the phone until she would have to tell me that she didn't have any money to send but that she would when she got her Social Security check next month. She rolled around her house in a wheelchair for those last few years and got to be a very funny person to talk to before she passed. It's only been a few months.

I am a firm believer in two aspects of emotional development in anyone who wants to get sober and more importantly, stay sober. Individual responsibility and forgiveness rank number one and two on the list but not necessarily in that order. Taking responsibility for your life is so important, because if you don't, then you are a victim. Please don't misunderstand. It's not to say that you have not suffered terrible grievances in life. Most people have in one way or another, but when we choose to blame someone else, we forfeit the power to get better. I blamed my father every second I was sick. The very instant I forgave him, that blame (or responsibility) fell on me. It gave me the power to overcome my addiction in so many ways, like forgiving him allowed me to receive forgiveness. If you're one of the chemically obsessed like I was, take a moment to see whom you blame instead of looking at yourself. Stop blaming others for your life, not because you're not justified in blaming them, but because you're only killing yourself. Unfortunately, while these points seem so obviously true and rational to the sane, addiction is an irrational disease, and those who suffer can't respond the way sane people do. Medical science mostly attributes it to psychological factors and at least one biological process (whatever that means). Twelve-Step programs say it is a spiritual disease, but both agree addiction is insanity.

Things with my mother and father are completely restored. They are better than they ever were. My mom is tickled that I haven't asked for money in more than four years, which along with ER visits, was something I spent an inordinate amount of time doing. She has been my greatest encourager in writing and has always believed in me.

Rufus Cumberbutt is a sort of pseudonym I invented for Facebook. It was under this name that I began to share some of the crazy things I wrote about my life. Many of the stories I tell are like pieces of shrapnel ripped into my mind and emotions over the years. Over the last two years they festered to the surface, so I pulled them out, cleaned them off and hand them to you now in this book. It is a collection of the oddly shaped artifacts which were once part of me. I hope you have appreciated them.

      I trained for a marathon this past summer and ran it Aug. 20 in North Bend, Washington. My father wanted to watch the total eclipse and since the path of totality lay somewhat close to where I lived in Idaho, he made plans to come up that weekend. When he showed up, I had already rented a hotel room for him, unlike every time he ever visited me before when I was homeless and strung out. It was so gratifying to tell him I had a room for him and pick him up in my own car from the Spokane airport. We visited some of my friends and drove to Seattle to meet my uncle.

      I ran the marathon on a Sunday, and I don't have to tell anyone who reads the Bible about the significance of running a race for your father. He handed out water at a station on the 20th mile and got to the finish line before I crossed it. It was one of the greatest moments of my life to be the man I had become and prove myself like that. My father witnessed it. Afterward, I puked a bunch, and we drove south for the rest of the day.

We watched the total eclipse in Lime, Oregon, on Monday morning and used Google maps to take a detour after we got through Baker City because of the traffic. The thin road wound back and forth through the small hills and passed through a piece of national forest and a town called Union before we got back on 84. There was more traffic around Pendleton, so we took another detour up through Walla Walla and north after that, covering 100 miles of rural road careening through hills of nothing but wheat. My father told me later that he'd never seen anything like it and that it was one of his favorite parts of the trip, but while we drove he insisted we were lost. A muttered curse word or two escaped his lips every 10 minutes, and he would ask me if I was sure about where we were going. We laughed at our predicament. Google Maps kept losing us. My father gripped the handle on the door and grunted. He needed a break from the ride.

The scenery changed briefly at a river and showed us an old sketchy bridge which we crossed to find ourselves at Lyons Ferry State Park. Tall green trees and grass sat against a large pool of the river, and ancient faces of brown and red rock stared at us from across a belly of the cold, dark water. They reminded us of how young we both still were. A child and his father played in the water close to us. The wife smoked a cigarette in her bathing suit at a picnic table. It was a great break from the ride, and we took this picture, just me and him on the river bank.

      I have learned a lot from what I have done and undone over the years of my life. I have learned that time passes, that moments are precious, and you can never get them back. Hate and fear will blind you. They will consume and kill you and everyone you love on the way. I know. I have seen it and lived it myself, but something tells me that I will spend the rest of my life trying to crawl back into that picture, back to the afternoon when we drove through those miserable fields of wheat together and laughed at being lost. This is what I learned: everything and everyone has a time limit. That means you and me and your kids, your worst enemy, even the smartest man in the world, and you can't get the time back no matter what you do.

THANK YOU

My gratitude is extended to many, too many to expect I will be able to remember them all. If you have ever told me that you liked what I've written on Reddit or Facebook or in real life and encouraged me, then you should know that I am so grateful for that and that your encouragement had a profound effect on me. Hopefully, the book wasn't a disappointment. I know many of you have had access to most all of what is written here, but the book puts things in order a little better and makes more sense of the whole story. Some people may not believe the story, but maybe its better that way.

If you liked the book and know anyone who might like to read it, pass it on, please.

DON'T DO DRUGS, PLEASE.

Your Friend,
Riley

Made in the USA
Monee, IL
10 April 2022